THE
Busy Moms
GUIDE TO
Writing

ANGELA CASTILLO
& JAMIE FOLEY

Copyright © 2018 Fayette Press

10 Digit ISBN: 0998207829
13 Digit ISBN: 978-0998207827
AISN: B0797HV4R7

Published in Bastrop, Texas

This novel is a work of fiction. Names, characters, places, and incidents are either used fictitiously or are products of the author's imagination. All characters are fictional, and any similarity to persons living or dead is coincidental.

Printed in the United States of America

Glossary

To the authors who helped us on our writing journeys

From inspiration to encouragement to hands-on help, we owe a great deal to those who've supported our writing careers. Jamie would like to thank Beth Wiseman for her steadfast faith in her career, even when it was about as promising a bullfrog auditioning for *The Voice*. Angela would like to thank Ryanna Fields, who believed in her writing and lifted her up like she has so many people over the years.

And of course, our amazing husbands and patient children enable us to embrace our creative sides with strength and excitement. We love you all so much.

To those who invested in making this book a success—our beta readers, editors, and proofers—thank you. You gave us confidence and joy in the knowledge that our failures and hard lessons learned were helpful to you.

And we are eternally grateful to the Creator who instilled us with our talents and passions, and brought us together for a friendship we cherish every day.

Chapter 1

YOU CAN DO THIS!
(NO, REALLY, YOU CAN!)

"For years, I have been a writing teacher who writes, trying to bring happiness to my students through literature. But all the while, I was also bringing happiness to myself through my life-long learning process of writing and telling stories."

— Audrey Wick, author of *Finding True North*

Supper should have been started half an hour ago, and a pile of laundry waits for you on the couch (well, it used to—now the kids have flung the clothes across the room in a free-for-all sock fight). Your baby is crying, and your oldest kid is yelling something about a science fair project being due tomorrow.

But what are you thinking about? A roving mercenary princess in your own made up land—the land of Flynn. You've dreamed about this land, pretended to live in it yourself. And more than anything, you want to *write* about it.

Your little girl grabs hold of your leg with sticky fingers. "Mommy, when are we going to have supper? I'm *hungry*, Mommy!"

If you're feeling tempted to check your home for a hidden camera, the reason we know these things is because we are there. We have nights like this on a continual basis. Yet between both of us, we have fifteen published books (and three collections). These books help to generate an income to help with grocery money and even, sometimes, the mortgage payment. Writing and Momming can happen! At the same time!

WHAT THIS BOOK WILL DO:

- Help you plan out your writing goals and time management
- Give you tools to do your personal best when it comes to writing
- Steer you away from mistakes we've made
- Encourage you to enlist aid from the right people—critique partners, editors, cover designers, and more
- Help you create a time budget, as well as a financial budget, so you don't go overboard
- Guide you to making the best decision for you regarding independent and traditional publishing
- Give you questions to ask yourself (and hopefully answer!) at the end of each chapter to help you move closer to your writing dreams

WHAT THIS BOOK *WON'T* DO:

- Teach you how to write a *New York Times* bestseller (if you find a book that can do this, let us know)
- Tell you to neglect your family in order to write
- Expect you to have a ten-thousand-dollar budget for your first book
- Tell you how to come up with writing ideas. There are countless other writing prompt books available out there. We figure if you picked up this book, you probably have ideas buzzing around in your head already and are looking for a way to let them out.
- Give you a magic formula to make millions of dollars with your books (we don't believe such a thing exists, but maybe. Of course, unicorns might exist too...)

Angela's Story

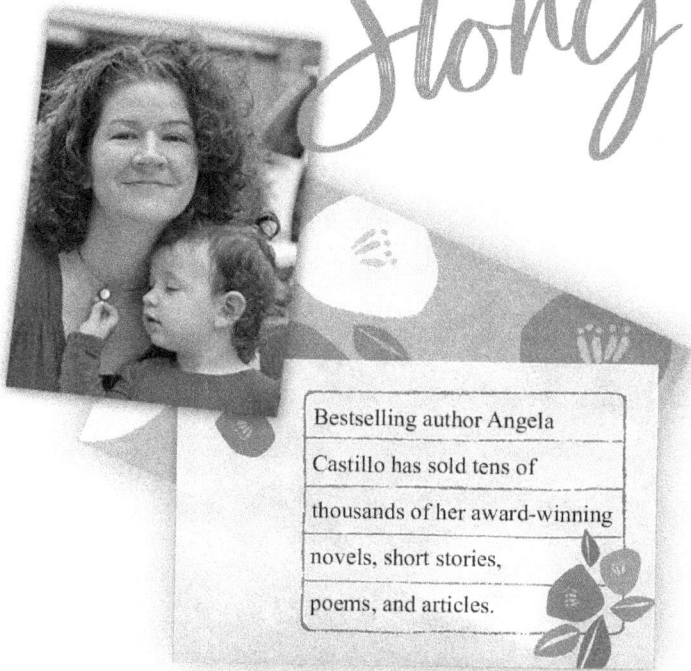

Bestselling author Angela Castillo has sold tens of thousands of her award-winning novels, short stories, poems, and articles.

My first story emerged from my yellow-green crayon at eight years old. By sixteen, every cent I could earn babysitting was spent on postage and envelopes to submit my poems, short stories and novels to any publishing company I could find. My first poem was published in a tiny literary journal, and I was hooked.

When I had my first child at the age of twenty-six, I thought I wouldn't have time to write anymore. Between working from home and motherhood, I didn't feel as though I had the brain space to write a grocery list, let alone organic creations anyone would be interested in reading.

But I missed writing. I began to design greeting cards for a print-on-demand site with my sister. I'd write the prose to go along with her photographs. The cards started to sell by the thousands, and customers gushed about how much they enjoyed the verses. I wrote freelance articles here and there, and pretty soon I was back in the swing of writing again.

Yes, it's a challenge to find the time to write, especially with four children now, but I've come to realize: writing is as much a part of who I am as being a mother.

Jamie's Story

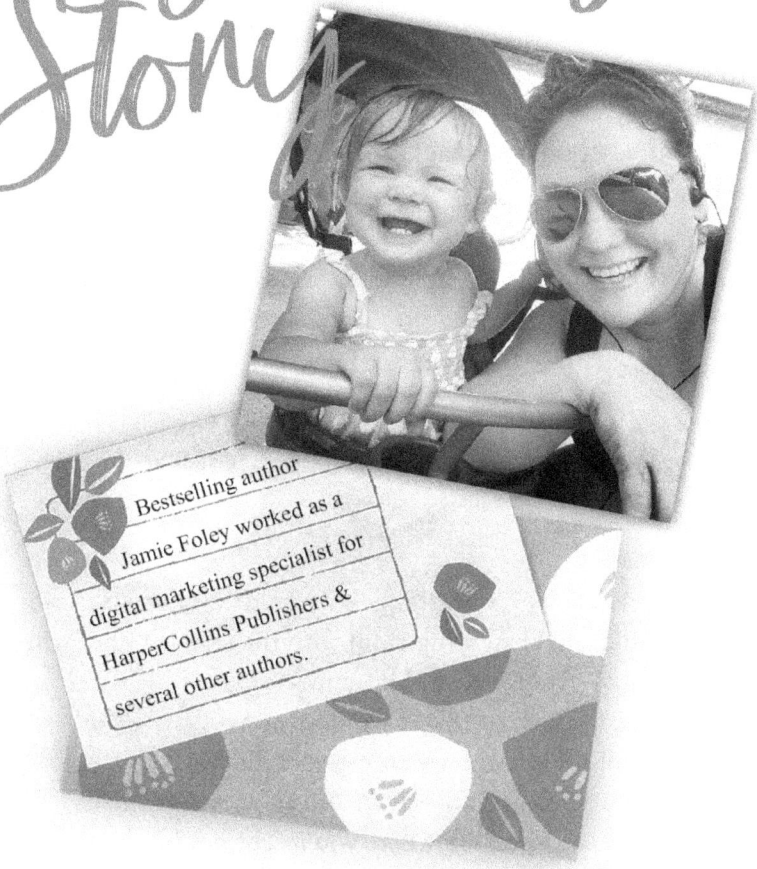

I started writing just before getting pregnant with my curly-haired, pony-loving girl, so it's always gone alongside motherhood for me. (But apparently I won the 'Storyteller Award' in second grade... not sure if that was for creativity or creative lying.)

When having a newborn flipped my naive life upside-down, I clung to writing to escape the sleep-deprived zombie mode. I wrote at midnight or three in the morning or through midday naps—whenever I could scrape the brain cells together. And it kept me sane through the NICU and a nasty car wreck I shouldn't have been able to walk away from.

Then we miscarried our second child. And our third.

My heart still aches as I write this, hoping to be able to keep the next baby. I know I'll never be the same, but writing has helped me to keep going through the grief and the constant mayhem of a vivacious toddler. Storytelling is a part of me—a facet of my soul—and writing is the creative expression that keeps me smiling during this beautifully chaotic phase of life.

Now please, don't get us wrong. We would never choose writing over our children. The crying child with the scraped knee will always get first priority over the next thousand words.

But we've discovered that if we stopped writing, we'd be stifling a very important part of who we are—a part that we couldn't just hide on a shelf until our children are grown and gone.

There are seasons of life where you might not be able to write. The last trimester of pregnancy, perhaps, or the month you volunteer to head up the PTA bake sale and everyone else decides to go on vacation the day of the event. Just as much as you need to write, you also need to give yourself permission to take breaks. But don't let these breaks last too long! It's important to keep motivated and—with whatever consistency you can squeeze out—to keep moving forward.

Becoming a mother doesn't mean we have to leave every other part of who we are behind—it just means we've added another layer to our soul and substance.

WHAT ARE YOUR WRITING EXPECTATIONS?

Like we said before, this book isn't a guarantee to bring you fame, fortune and *Twilight*-like success. But we can encourage you to progress in your writing journey and guide you along the way.

We're not saying it's impossible to have success as a writer—there are hundreds of writer moms out there who are contributing to the family income with their work, us included. But the first goal in our writing should be to have a positive outlet, to express ourselves in a way that gives us creative fulfillment. It can be a way to unwind and relax, which in turn will make us better moms.

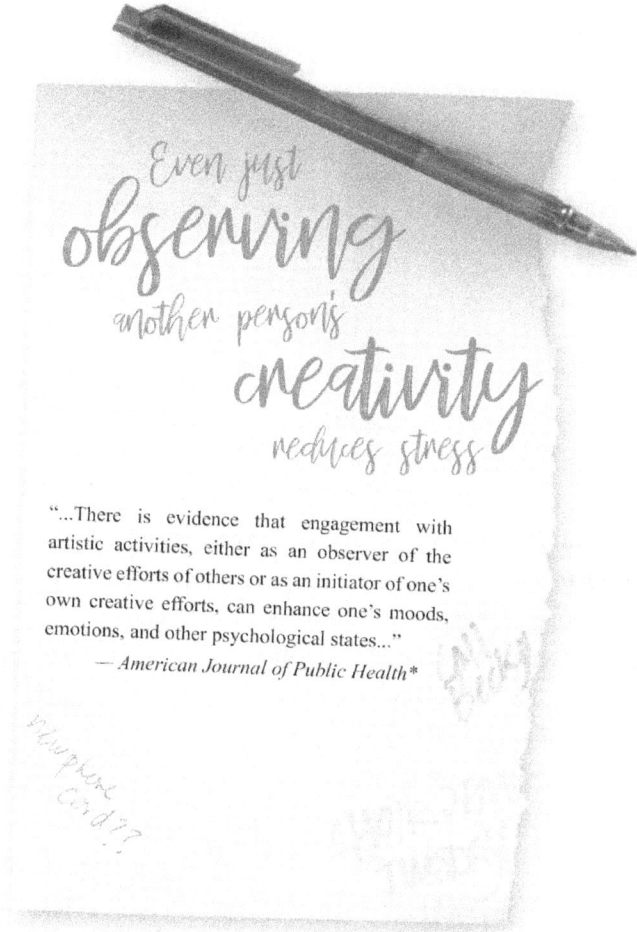

Even just **observing** *another person's* **creativity** *reduces stress*

"...There is evidence that engagement with artistic activities, either as an observer of the creative efforts of others or as an initiator of one's own creative efforts, can enhance one's moods, emotions, and other psychological states..."
— *American Journal of Public Health**

The first thing to determine is *why* you want to write. Could it be:

FOR YOURSELF ONLY

- Daily thoughts or poems
- A prayer journal
- Burn letters to work through conflict
- Chore lists and household planning

FOR A FEW OTHER PEOPLE

- Baby books or scrapbooks
- Letters or emails
- Memory books—your memoir or that of your ancestors
- Bedtime stories you told your kids that you want to pass on, or a children's book written for your descendants
- A cookbook of family recipes

TO BE SHARED WITH AS MANY PEOPLE AS POSSIBLE

- Blogs
- Fanfiction
- Self-help books
- Freelance articles, short stories, and poems for literary magazines
- Fiction books written with intent to profit

Of course, many writers work in some or all of these categories, but it's important to decide on priorities, and to be aware of the investment required for reaching each audience. For instance, if you want time to write handwritten letters a few times a month, it's obviously not going to take as much thought and time as a hundred-thousand-word epic fantasy (unless you're a unicorn).

If you simply want stories to share with family members or friends, you may not want to put thousands of dollars into binding, editing, et cetera. The great thing is, you *can* do a project like this, and you don't have to spend a ton of money on it. We'll get into budget and cost expectations

CHECK OUT THE

Busy Moms:

GUIDE TO

Novel Marketing

IF YOU CRAVE MORE DETAILS REGARDING BUDGETING AND INCOME.

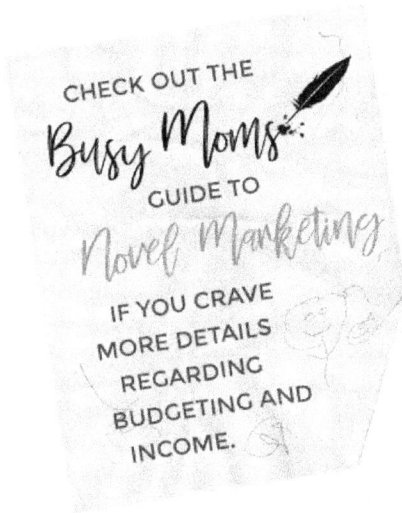

(as well as *profit* expectations) in Chapter 10: The Next Steps.

Regardless of which path you choose, the most important thing is to take time to write consistently. We'll cover *how* to make time between diaper changes and soccer practice in the next chapter.

QUESTIONS:

1. What do I want to write?
2. Who do I want to share it with?
3. Who can I help along this creative journey, and who can encourage me in return?

Chapter 2

GOALS FOR WORLD DOMINATION

(OR SURVIVING UNTIL YOUR
YOUNGEST KID'S 6TH BIRTHDAY PARTY)

"In five years, I hope to have at least one book that really 'takes off.' I'd like to continue building a kids' series... I also enjoy writing fiction (I'm working on my second fiction novel), so I'd love to see that multiply and expand."

— Traci Vanderbush, author of *Porches of Holly*

Even if we set goals, we don't always keep them. They can be intimidating and might infringe on our Netflix time and normally involve some kind of math. Ew.

And besides, our kids are masters at rearranging our schedules when we least expect it. Virus picked up at school, anyone?

According to a study by Dominican University*, people who write their goals down are 50% more likely to achieve their goals than those who don't. And of course we want you to be successful, so we encourage you to determine goals, even if it gives you a momentary headache. You can have an extra piece of dark chocolate to make up for it. We'll wait while you go find one.

A writer's goals will naturally vary by the purpose for writing, the time available for writing (check out Chapter 3 for ideas on finding time to write), what length of story is being written, and the genre that has been chosen. Your goals will need to reflect what's most important to you and create a comfortable yet disciplined framework that will drive you toward achieving your dreams.

HOW LONG WILL YOUR BOOK BE?

Did you do your homework from the end of Chapter 1? We know, last night's dinner resulted in a new shade of spaghetti sauce on the wall, so you had other priorities. But do you know the answer to the question, "What do I want to write?"

If you're only writing for yourself or a few people and have no expectations for making a profit, you don't really have to worry about length. Write until the story is done and be happy.

But there are some things to consider if you are writing with future sales in mind. Publishers, agents, and your target readers will expect your book to be a certain length, depending on its genre.

Deciding on a genre will help you estimate how long your book will be, and therefore, how much time you'll need to write it. Here are the average lengths of books in different genres (please note: these are just averages from *Writer's Digest**):

- **Adult Fiction, including Literary, Mainstream, Women's, Romance, Mystery, Suspense, Thriller, & Horror:** 80,000 - 90,000 words
- **Chick Lit:** 70,000 - 75,000 words
- **Science Fiction & Fantasy:** 100,000 - 115,000 words
- **Westerns:** 50,000 - 80,000 words
- **Memoir:** 80,000 - 90,000 words
- **Young Adult (targeted to ages 12-18):** 55,000 - 80,000 words

- **Middle Grade (targeted to ages 8-12):** 20,000 - 55,000 words
- **Picture Books:** 500 - 600 words

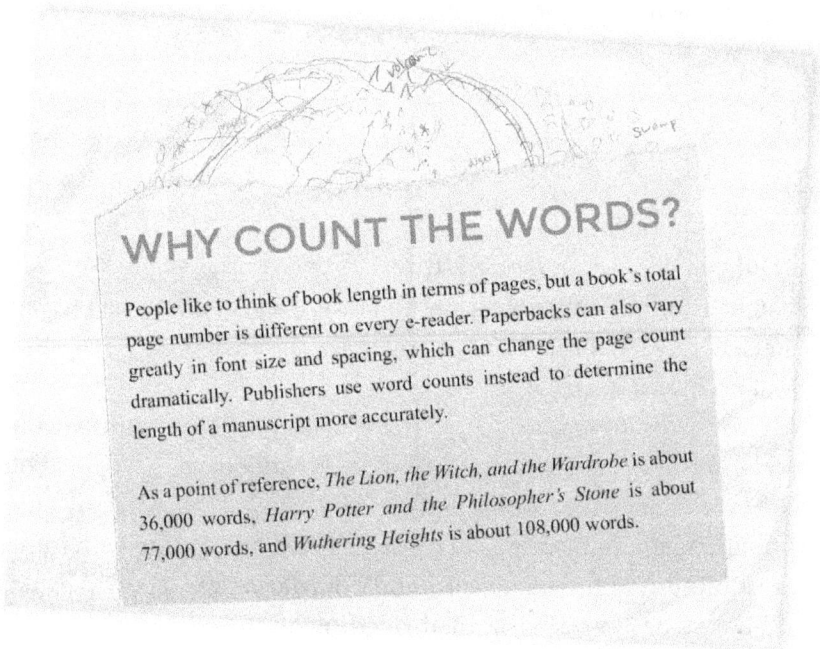

WHY COUNT THE WORDS?

People like to think of book length in terms of pages, but a book's total page number is different on every e-reader. Paperbacks can also vary greatly in font size and spacing, which can change the page count dramatically. Publishers use word counts instead to determine the length of a manuscript more accurately.

As a point of reference, *The Lion, the Witch, and the Wardrobe* is about 36,000 words, *Harry Potter and the Philosopher's Stone* is about 77,000 words, and *Wuthering Heights* is about 108,000 words.

Want to write something shorter? Here are the categorizations of book lengths (of course, different sources will give you different lengths, so these aren't set in stone. These are from the Nebula Awards®*):

- **Short story:** less than 7,500 words
- **Novelette:** 7,500 - 17,500 words
- **Novella:** 17,500 - 40,000 words
- **Novel:** 40,000+ words

Please keep in mind: Short stories are a great way to practice writing and can actually be more complicated than novels to plot and trim to perfection. However, they can be tricky to market. Not very many people have made millions on short stories, but on the other hand, not too many folks have made millions selling books in general. If you think you might like it, give it a shot!

BREAK IT DOWN

Once you know your book's targeted length, break down how long it will take to complete based on how many words you want to write per work day. Here are some examples:

70,000-word contemporary romance novel
500 words per weekday
= 11,000 words per month, 7 months until rough draft is completed

35,000-word novella
1,000 words per weekday
= 22,000 words per month, 1.5 months until rough draft is completed

5,000-word short story
250 words per weekday
= 20 days until rough draft is completed

If you are a spreadsheet sort of person, you might consider creating one to help you with your goals. Or do what Angela does and write down your goals on a giant desk calendar, with your word count on each day of the week. Angela gets extreme satisfaction from crossing out each day, knowing she's completed her word count. (Of course, this can also go south very quickly if Angela does not get her word count completed for the day. But we digress.)

To series or not to series?

Most authors agree that sales go up when they add books to a series. This is especially true of genre fiction such as sci-fi, fantasy, and romance.

This is because readers of these genres tend to be voracious, and when they see a series that looks promising, they tend to buy the whole set in one fell swoop.

It's a lovely habit, don't you think?

BE SPECIFIC

Now that you have an idea of what type of book you want to write, where do you want to be in 10 years (besides your kids reaching the magical age where they do all of the housework, or you become a vacation-hopping empty nester)?

Don't be afraid to reach for your wildest dreams. Do you want to have your first book published, or just written? How many books—are they a part of a series, or a collection of short stories or novellas? Be specific.

From this 10-year mark you can break down the steps needed to accomplish your goal. What do you need to have accomplished at the 5-year mark? Break that down further to determine where you need to be 1 year from now.

Then bust up this year's goal into 12 months. From there, divide the work into weeks, and finally into weekdays.

Just stick to your schedule, and before you know it, your dreams will be reality. Even if you fall short, you'll still be better off than when you started!

If this sounds *way* too complicated and terrifying, stick with us for an example from Jamie's schedule.

Jamie's calendar

Jamie has a ridiculous 12-month calendar taking up her husband's entire office wall. She uses it for writing goals and marketing scheduling, but she's probably more OCD than you, so don't be intimidated. Having everything planned out is stress-relieving for her, because she knows if she can just meet today's goals, she'll be on track for meeting that 10-year endgame.

EXAMPLE: JAMIE'S GOALS

As a fantasy writer, Jamie tends to write huge, complicated books that take almost as much time to plan as they do to write. She's halfway through her 10-year plan, so let's take a look at the breakdown.

1-year goal: Outline and finish her first book, *Sentinel.*

5-year goal: Learn the craft of writing, establish a marketing platform (website, email newsletter list, and social media), and publish the 3-novel *The Sentinel Trilogy.*

10-year goal: Master the craft of writing, publish 2 more fantasy series, make at least $30,000/year in writing income, and learn to make the best low-carb chocolate chip cookies the galaxy has ever beheld.

Jamie has just achieved her first 5-year goal (woohoo!), so let's break down her 6th-year goals.

YEAR 6:
- Write and edit 3 novels to begin new fantasy series
- Complete 3 outlines for next year's books
- Expand fanbase with at least 3 marketing promotions each month
- Attend at least 1 writer's conference
- Read at least 3 new books on the craft of writing
- Read at least 5 bestselling books within her genre
- Discover an ancient Mayan secret, revealing how to make the best low-carb cookies the denizens of Earth have ever beheld

See how specific these are? OK, don't count the Mayan secret.

Now that we have specific numbers associated with each goal, they can be broken down into months, and from there, daily goals.

Let's bust the year into 9 months of work (excluding summer months for fun with the kiddos and December for holidays). Jamie's books tend to be about 80,000 words each, so writing three books means she'll need to schedule time for writing 240,000 words over 9 months.

240,000 words / 9 months = 26,667 words per month

Sweet! Now, Jamie only writes 4 days per week, because kids happen (and random holidays and tornadoes and ninja attacks). That makes about 16 work days per month.

26,667 words / 16 work days per month = 1,667 words per day

Now, this is probably too many words per day to schedule for a beginning writer (especially a busy mom), but it's a cozy goal for Jamie, now that she's practiced full-time writing for 5 years. She'll also have to squeeze in time for outlining, editing, and marketing. Since one of her writing sessions only takes about 2-3 hours, that'll be no problemo.

New writers will need to factor in more time for editing and writing second, third, or ninth drafts (doubling or tripling your writing time is a good rule of thumb). Use this system to create a plan that's perfect for you!

And don't forget to schedule a few days for margarita breaks. Everybody needs margarita breaks.

TIPS FOR DEVELOPING YOUR EPIC PLAN

BUDGET TIME TO LEARN AND GROW

Nobody starts off writing bestselling material (sorry), so give yourself at least a year to practice and learn the craft. It took Jamie 3 years to consider herself a halfway decent writer, and another 2 years of editing, rewriting, reading craft books, and attending conferences to become confident in her writing ability (and she still has a long way to go). Schedule yourself plenty of time to practice and learn!

Even though Mozart was a prodigy, he didn't become a master overnight—no one does. If you try to publish your first book without any education on the craft, practice, or professional editing, it's going to look more like your kindergartner's finger painting rather than a masterpiece to readers, literary agents, and publishers.

DON'T FORGET EDITING TIME

Double your writing time—that's probably how long the second and third draft edits will take. This may take longer if you have a critique group to help you out, since you'll be waiting on feedback from other people. And most critique groups depend on critique trades, so you could be spending some of your editing time critiquing other people's work. (More on that in Chapters 6 and 7.) Of course, everyone is different—this is just a standard approximation and could be different for you. After you've completed a few books, you'll get a better idea of how long your editing process will take.

If you are planning on going indie (self-publishing), you'll also need to factor in time for formatting and cover development, but we'll cover that in Chapter 9 and *The Busy Mom's Guide to Indie Publishing*.

BE AN AWESOME BOSS

Sometimes we can be meaner bosses to ourselves than we would ever be to another person. Don't be too harsh on yourself when you miss a deadline—sometimes life happens. Just get right back on the horse.

Reward yourself for hitting your goals. Did you hit your word goal for the week? Someone deserves a bowl of Blue Bell ice cream. Did you finish that outline on time? Well now, have yourself a pedicure. Finished a book? Spa time. You deserve it.

ITTY-BITTY GOALS

If you're like Angela, and don't have the brain power to even consider life 10 years ahead, we recommend starting a bit smaller. You can start with a 2-year plan. Or even a 2-month plan if you want to attempt publishing a short story. Maybe you'd like to commit to reading one craft book a month, or just be able to write something every day, even if it is a note to your child's teacher. Small goals are OK, but once you become disciplined to follow through with those, try for something higher.

DON'T BE INTIMIDATED!

After you've figured out how much time you will be able to write every day, (and finished the last few bites of Rocky Road), make sure the breakdown of your 10-year goal aligns with reality, and adjust where needed to give yourself some padding. For some people, goals can be intimidating, but remember, this is for your sake. This is to help you get in a writing habit so you can accomplish your writing dream. You are a writing *princess!* (Or superhero. Or Wonder Woman, who is both a princess and superhero, and personally our favorite.)

This technique of making goals and time management won't work for everyone. Work to develop a system that works for you. Just make sure you're moving forward in a disciplined manner if the dream of becoming a writer is truly important to you.

Just think of it: in a year or less, you could have a book pretty much finished. Instead of thinking every day, "Wow, I wish I could write. I wish I could share this amazing story I have in my head," you will have it in your hand. Or on your hard drive, at least!

Make your goals possible, and you will be successful. Be honest with yourself. If you want an hour to write every day, but know it's probably going to be more like 20 minutes, start with 20 minutes. That way you can reach your goal every day. It's more important to keep going at a steady pace rather than aiming too high and sinking down into feelings of failure right off the bat.

In the next chapter, we'll brainstorm about how to find time to write even in the busiest mom's life.

QUESTIONS:

1. What are my 10, 5, and 1-year writing goals?
2. Which friends can I call on for support and accountability during my writing journey?
3. Where can I display my goals so they can encourage me, rather than being overlooked or forgotten?

Chapter 3

FINDING TIME TO WRITE

"*I set up our house so that my office is right next to my kids' playroom. Most days, I usually try to sit down right after breakfast and do some writing. Doing it first thing like this helps me get it done every day. I've also trained my kids to know that when mom's at her desk, they need to let me work. Setting a timer on my phone helps—I use an app so that I work for 20 minutes, then have a 5 minute break. My boys know when they hear the timer on my phone go off, they can come bug me for a few minutes about getting a drink or a snack.*"

— H. A. Titus, author of *Forged Steel*

One of the most important things to determine as a writing mom is when you're going to write. We want to stress (again), we're not encouraging you to choose writing over your children or your spouse. Of course, they come first. But you should also have time to for your art. Everyone needs time for creative expression.

The amount of time will vary, of course, by the writer and purpose for writing. If you want time to write a children's book, that's a much different stretch of time than writing a romantic suspense novel.

CARVING OUT TIME IN AN ALREADY JAM-PACKED SCHEDULE

As Angela is typing up this book, she has just finished making supper, which happens to be frozen lasagna. She's been chasing her busy (and death-defying) one-year-old all over the house. Though she's been doing dishes all day, there's still a teetering pile in the sink. But lo and behold, her baby is down for a nap, so she's typing feverishly, trying to get a little bit done for the day. Every word is a triumph at this season of life.

We know it can be really difficult to find time to write. Remember, some writing is better than nothing. So if you only have fifteen minutes a day at first, that's all right.

Think about the things you accomplish every day. You get your children fed. You do the laundry and the dishes. You run errands and go grocery shopping. Somehow, even though you're busy, you make time for them. Why? Because they are important. They are priorities. So if you want to have time to write, you have to make it an important part of your day. Otherwise it will keep being placed on the back burner of your time until the day is gone and you're already asleep. (Or being woken up ten times. Whichever.)

SOME IDEAS FOR FINDING TIME TO WRITE:

- **Wake up thirty minutes earlier** than your kids normally get up, or stay up thirty minutes later than usual.
- **Don't check any social media** until you've written your quota for the day.
- **Purchase an inexpensive document app** for your phone (or use

Google Drive for free) and type on your phone/tablet instead of playing app games while you're in line at the grocery store or waiting in the doctor's office.

- **Bring a notebook into the playroom** and write while your child is busy with toys. (Some people can also write on their phone or tablet, but it's not for everyone).
- **Hire a responsible teenager** from the neighborhood to play with your children for a short amount of time while you write in another room.
- **Save some of the kids' TV time** for when you want to write.
- **Work out a specific day** and amount per week with your partner for you to take your laptop or tablet to a coffee shop or park and write. This is NOT a selfish thing to ask for. Trade time off, if needed.
- **Trade babysitting** with other moms who also want time to create. This can really work out well for moms with kids of similar ages.

Once you've carved out your writing time and you're sitting there, in your little writing space, *don't waste it!* Stay away from social media. Turn off your phone. Don't look around at housework or paperwork that needs to be done. And no matter what, don't think about the leftover ice cream in the freezer.

Never mind... some distractions are too important to ignore. You can write while eating ice cream, right? You have our permission.

CREATE A CONDUCIVE WRITING ENVIRONMENT AT HOME

Some people can tone out messes, screaming children, noisy pets, and everything else in between. But sometimes it helps to create a writing environment. A sort of way to trigger your brain into 'writing mode.'

You might be chuckling to yourself, thinking it's hard enough to go to the bathroom when your kids are home, let alone have a space to yourself. But you can find simple ways to set apart your place.

- **Play soft music in the background.** YouTube has hundreds of music mixes to choose from. Jamie is distracted by music with lyrics, but she loves to listen to ambient sounds similar to the setting of the scene she's writing. Check out www.mynoise.net for some awesome ambience.
- **Choose a comfortable chair.** Maybe if you work with a laptop or a tablet you could even purchase a beanbag chair. If the weather's nice, set up a place outside.
- **Light a candle** nearby or use a diffuser with essential oils.
- **Hang pictures** you like on the walls around you, or use a colorful scarf as a cover for your computer desk. At the very least, pick a pleasant, inspiring background photo for your screen.
- **Gather a few objects** from around the house that inspire you and place them in your writing space. Maybe a pretty vase, a figurine from a family member, or an antique picture frame. Or maybe a live fern or a hanging vine.

The most important thing about your writing space is making it a place that is comfortable, inspiring, and a place you are drawn to—a place where you *want* to be.

WHEN YOU CAN ESCAPE THE HOUSE: FINDING THE BEST PLACES TO WRITE

Sometimes the TV, the laundry or Pinterest can be a bit too distracting. If you find yourself randomly yelling, "Squirrel!" like Jamie, you might benefit from getting out of the house every once in awhile.

But if you can escape, where should you go? Some writers prefer background noise, so coffee shops or bookstores could make great writing locations (you might even score a power outlet for your laptop).

Or if you need peace and quiet, find picnic benches at your local parks, weather permitting, or your local library. Some libraries have quiet rooms you can request.

Genre-specific locations can also be great environments. If you write science fiction or fantasy, this might be your local game store. If you write historicals, it might be landmarks or museums.

If you're on vacation, and writing is relaxing for you, snuggle up on your hotel balcony or courtyard. And of course, some tourist spots like a beach or lakeside can be very inspiring!

"I go through seasons with writing. There are periods of time when I don't write much at all, but ponder things in my mind and in conversations with God. I have seasons when writing is unstoppable and I get in a flow. In those moments, I write daily until I hit a moment when I know it's time to 'set the pen down' and listen."

TRACI VANDERBUSH
Writer & Evangelist

BALANCING YOUR FAMILY AND YOUR WRITING

INVOLVING YOUR CREATIVE KIDDOS

For the most part, writing time should be your time, but there are ways to include your family as well. If you're writing a children's story, read it out loud to your kids and ask for input. You never know what valuable ideas they might come up with.

Ask them to draw a costume for a character, come up with an animal's name, or paint your created planet on a paper plate. Who knows—their refrigerator-worthy artwork may be inspirational for you.

Bring up scenarios from your story (only if age appropriate, of course) and ask your children what they would do in that situation. If you are trying to choose a cover from several options your graphic design artist has sent you, ask them which one they like the best. Most kids love being consulted about story details and love when their ideas are included.

GETTING YOUR SIGNIFICANT OTHER ON BOARD

We have both been extremely blessed to have loving spouses that support our writing in every way. But in some relationships it may take a bit of discussion for a spouse to see why writing is so important to you. And that's OK.

We do not recommend you hide your writing from your spouse or allow it to get in the way of your relationship.

However, if this becomes a huge issue of conflict, you might need to meet with a counselor or pastor to talk things through. Don't let any negative person—even a spouse—keep you from a creative, healthy exercise that you feel called to do. Of course we love others and respect their needs and desires, but we need to be respected too.

HARD DAYS WILL COME

Every writer has those days where they begin to doubt themselves and wonder why they even thought this would be a good idea. For Angela, this usually happens somewhere in the middle of the third draft, when the shine has worn off the new project. It's OK to put everything aside for a day or two and do something else productive with your little niche of time, like, oh, rewatching the first five episodes of *Gilmore Girls.* But don't let it happen too often. Keep a paper with your goals written on it taped up next to your writing space, and remember no 100,000 page epic fantasy was written in a day. These things take time, but they *can* happen.

CHANGES IN FAMILY DYNAMICS

Sometimes things unexpectedly change and our writing dynamic gets completely thrown off. This recently happened to Angela, who was blessed with a wonderful surprise: a baby boy. Before, she was able to do her writing at night when the children were in bed, but the new baby proved to be a night owl who didn't want to go to bed early. She found herself typing fewer and fewer words every night, and the ones she did type made little sense when she'd read them over the next day.

But even though her baby stayed up late, he'd sleep in. So she realized if she changed her writing time to the morning, she could get in an hour or so of writing before everyone else woke up. She'd go to bed with the baby and wake up with at least 7 hours of sleep under her belt the next morning. And her writing quantity and quality improved immensely. Sometimes if your plan stops working, you have to be willing to change it up. Try a change before you give up completely.

A NOTE ON HEALTH

Please keep this in mind as you are making your goals and plans. Don't forget the reason why they tell adults to put the oxygen masks on first in a plane before helping children with theirs: If you don't get enough rest, you won't be your best for your family or yourself. So while writing is important and should be a priority, it's not more important than your health.

Don't bog yourself down. Don't allow yourself to lose your joy.

Also, if you have plans to make money with your writing and use it to help bring in a partial income, please make sure you have realistic expectations. It can take time, up to a few years, to get a manuscript accepted and published (and even if you're self-publishing it can take awhile). Give yourself time to get these things done and don't allow yourself to get stressed out about it. After all, this is supposed to be fun!

QUESTIONS:

1. Where would be the best place for me to write?
2. How can I create the best possible writing environment?
3. What can I sacrifice to find 30 minutes of writing time per workday?

Chapter 4

PLOTTING YOUR STORY
LIKE AN EVIL MASTERMIND

"I think [my children] keep me fresh. Kids live in a world of constant possibilities. I try to embrace that sense of exploration and wonder in my work."

— H. L. Burke, author of the *Nyssa Glass* series

A TALE OF TWO GARDENERS

There once were two neighbors who loved to grow vegetables and herbs and flowers of every kind. One crafted a greenhouse, planning every angle and hinge, while her neighbor simply scattered seeds in a fertile bed.

"You'll never grow proper plants without planning," the first gardener said as she marked off a foot-long square for her green onions.

The second gardener sniffed as he drizzled organic fertilizer over his soil. "You're missing the natural beauty of growth without nurturing your seedlings!"

We grow our stories similarly, either by plotting every last detail or pantsing—writing by the seat of our pants.

Plotters design meticulous outlines, planning what will happen and using methods like pre-writing to control their story's twists and turns. Plotting is particularly advantageous to non-fiction writers and writers of genres with complicated storylines like science fiction, epic fantasy, thriller, or mystery.

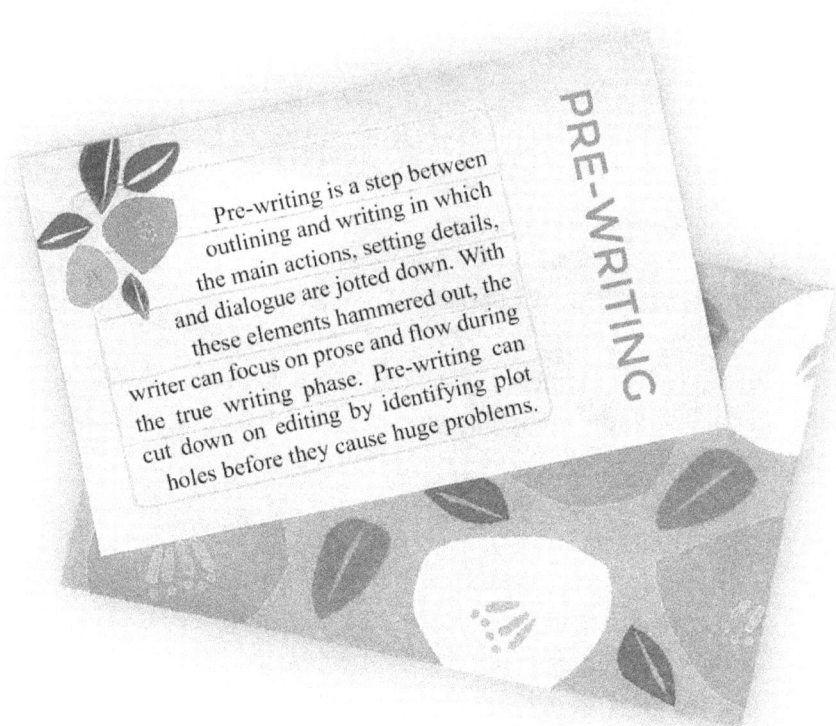

PRE-WRITING

Pre-writing is a step between outlining and writing in which the main actions, setting details, and dialogue are jotted down. With these elements hammered out, the writer can focus on prose and flow during the true writing phase. Pre-writing can cut down on editing by identifying plot holes before they cause huge problems.

Pantsers nurture their characters and let them guide the story without a solid plan in place—but they may have a general idea of how they want things to end up. This type of writing may feel more natural. Pantsing might be a better option for emotionally-driven stories, including romance, women's fiction, and artistic writing. But of course, it depends on the writer's personal preference.

Most writers land somewhere in the middle, and may change their methods depending on the project or at different points in their career. J.K. Rowling and John Grisham are well-known plotters, while Stephen King and George R.R. Martin are notorious pantsers.

If you're a pantser, far be it from us to tell you how to express yourself through your writing (although Angela has some tips later on in this chapter). But if you love your outlines as much as Jamie does, we've got a tip or two.

PLOTTING: JAMIE'S METHOD

THE PLOT EQUATION

If you can condense your story idea into a single sentence or two, it can go a long way toward focusing your writing goals. It'll also help out later when pitching your book to agents or publishers, or developing back cover copy.

There are five elements that compose a basic plot equation: the inciting incident, the main character, the objective, the antagonist, and the climax.

Let's take Jamie's urban fantasy novel, *Vanguard,* as an example:

> *When terrorists attack Brazen Tower, Jet Valinor joins a special ops unit to ensure justice is done. But when the terrorists' lead supporter, Ari Qua'set, orchestrates betrayal within Viper Unit, Jet must rely on a foreign slave for survival.*

This example breaks down like so:

- **Inciting Incident:** When terrorists attack Brazen Tower,
- **Main Character:** Jet Valinor

- **Objective:** joins a special ops unit to ensure justice is done. But when
- **Antagonist:** the terrorists' lead supporter, Ari Qua'set,
- **Climax:** orchestrates betrayal within Viper Unit, Jet must rely on a foreign slave for survival.

Inciting Incident: The beginning of your equation might include a hint of your setting to give the reader a little flavor right from the get-go. But more importantly, the inciting incident illustrates the event that really kicks off your story—even if you feel like it's a spoiler.

Main Character: You might have more than one important character, but someone always takes the lead. The main character tends to be the most affected by the situation, and maintains the primary drive toward the climax. If you have two primary POVs with separate objectives, write a unique plot equation for each of them.

Objective: Your main character's goal. After the inciting incident, what do they do to try and fix their problem?

Antagonist: The 'bad guy' doesn't necessarily have to be a single person. It could be a situation or an environment or an internal struggle. Whatever the opponent is, make sure it isn't weak! Defining your main character's opponent here will help to form an idea of your story goals.

Climax: The most intense or dangerous portion of your plot—the final showdown between your main character and their struggle.

Play around with your story and this equation until you feel you have a compelling, unique idea. When you've got something you're confident in, share it with some friends and ask for their honest opinion. If they enjoy books in the same genre, would they pick up the book if they read your plot equation on the back cover?

Once you've got a solid equation down, it's time to move on to the outline!

THE ANATOMY OF A WELL-STRUCTURED OUTLINE

Every genre is different, but this illustration of a skeleton may help you devise a general organization for your unique story.

THE PLOT SKELETON

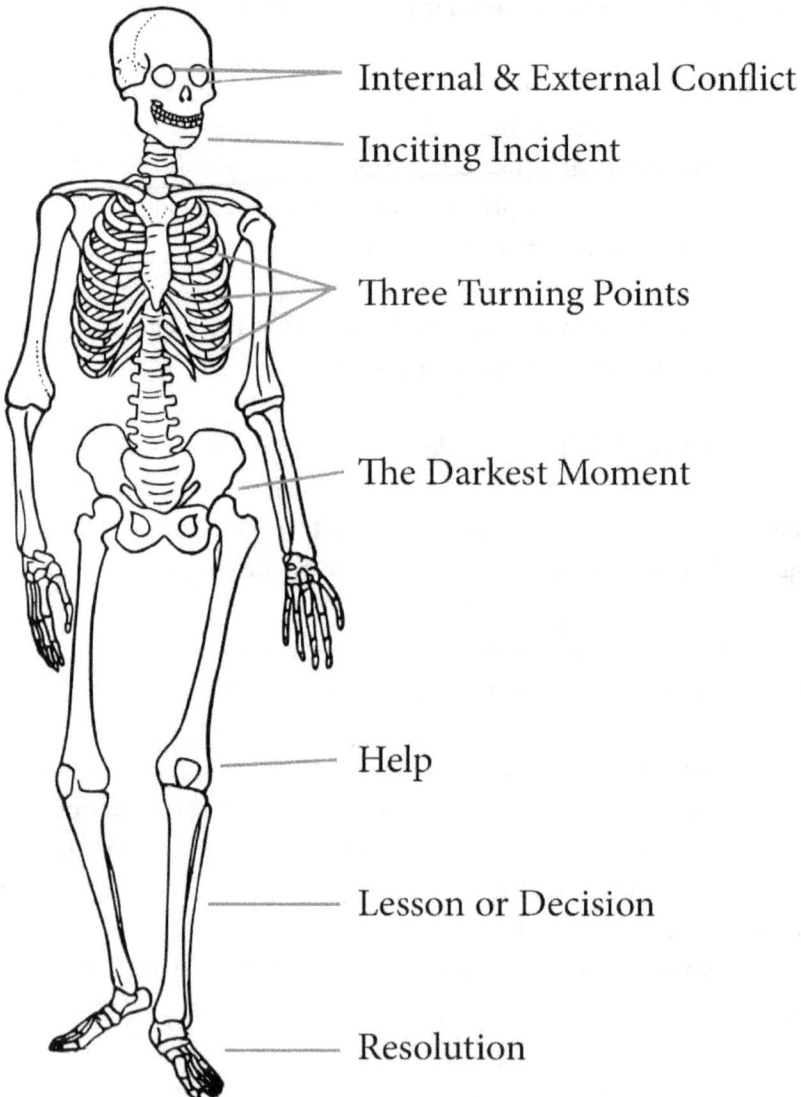

Internal & External Conflict

Inciting Incident

Three Turning Points

The Darkest Moment

Help

Lesson or Decision

Resolution

TWO EYES: THE INTERNAL & EXTERNAL CONFLICT

Your main character should have two problems to overcome: their internal (or hidden) conflict, and the external (or obvious) need. They are both equally important, and should be resolved by the end of the story.

In *Romeo and Juliet,* the external conflict is two families at each other's throats. Meanwhile, Romeo and Juliet's internal struggles put their own flesh and blood against their love.

CHIN: INCITING INCIDENT

The inciting incident is the event that catapults your main character onto their main quest. In *Harry Potter and the Sorcerer's Stone,* this happens when Harry receives a letter inviting him to Hogwarts. The inciting incident needs to happen soon after the story begins to maintain your reader's attention.

THREE RIBS: TURNING POINTS

Turning points are when your main character tries to accomplish their goal—to resolve one of their conflicts—and fails. These events compose the middle bulk of your story.

RUMP: THE DARKEST MOMENT

When your main character is knocked on their behind, you've probably reached the darkest moment. This could be the death of a loved one or the loss of something irreplaceable. All hope seems lost.

KNEES: HELP

Your character hits their knees, reeling from the darkest moment. This is where someone comes to their aid, offering encouragement, wisdom, or a new weapon to resolve the conflict.

BOOTSTRAPS: LESSON OR DECISION

Pull yourself up by your bootstraps! Armed with new aid, your character charges forward and faces their conflicts.

FEET: RESOLUTION

The battle is over. Now is the time for your internal and external conflicts to be resolved—whether or not your character actually succeeded as originally intended. Form your happily ever after and write 'The End!'

PANTSING: ANGELA'S METHOD

Angela wouldn't say she never plots anything. She does quite a bit of pre-writing for her books, but much of her story flows out in the moment of writing, and things change on a whim. For example, one of the characters in a historical romance she wrote was only supposed to appear for five minutes. She ended up running off with the main character's group, becoming a bigger side character... and in the end, she got her own book.

The way Angela usually come up with stories is by telling them to herself on long car trips when she's alone. With four kids, it's really the only time she has long stretches to think. If you want to try this method, you could record yourself on your phone or a small tape recorder. (Wait, does anyone even know what those are anymore? Better go with your phone.)

JUST GET IT OUT

Angela writes a story like you'd mix a salad. She chops everything up, throws it in a bowl, and if it looks like she needs to add more of something, she adds more. She prefers to let creative ideas flow as they will.

But she must hurry and get the ideas out, or they begin to wilt, brown, and suddenly they've rotted away, to be pushed to the back of the refrigerator, never to be seen again. (Of course, her refrigerator in real life is spotless. She would never dream of leaving anything in there long enough to rot. But back to pantsing.)

The idea of carefully planning out a novel makes Angela's eyes glaze over and her brain feel like her kid put it in the microwave. If you're like Angela, just ignore Jamie's meticulous take-over-the-world plots and move forward.

NOVELETTE, NOVELLA, NOVEL... WHAT?

Once you have an idea of how long your story will be—whether you're plotting or pantsing—you might have an idea of *chapter* count, but that still doesn't give you a calculation of your *word* count. We discussed this to some extent in chapter 2, but we'll expound on it a bit. The final word count for your story is going to matter for many reasons.

- Readers of different genres are going to expect books of different sizes. For instance, romance readers might be looking for a light, quick read (sometimes referred to as a 'beach read'). This could be anywhere from novelette size to a shorter novel, around 60,000 words. These books can be great sellers because their buyers read through them quickly, and then search through Amazon for more. On the other hand, an epic fantasy can run 120,000 words or more. Fantasies are fun to write, but can be time consuming.

- If you plan to submit your book to a traditional publisher, they are going to expect certain word counts for certain genres. On the other hand, if you self-publish, you will not be able to charge as much (most of the time) for a novella as for a longer novel. Of course, there are always exceptions to this rule.

- When you're marketing your book, some book promotion sites do not accept stories shorter than a certain length. Keep this in mind for the future.

If your book is running too long, you can always consider breaking it up into two or more books. Several books are almost always better than one.

THE ADVANTAGES OF SERIES

Angela never planned for her book, *The River Girl's Song,* to be the beginning of a series. But as she developed her book, she became very fond of a side character, Soonie. Angela decided she wanted to know more about Soonie, so she began to jot down ideas for the next installation in the series. When Angela launched *River Girl,* she realized more and more the value of having follow up books for readers to purchase (this creates a much more profitable situation for the author). So she was glad to have the notes when she was ready to write the next book.

Sometimes deciding to continue with a series is like deciding whether or not to have another kid. Sure, it's painful, and it takes a lot of time and energy, but in the end, it's also very rewarding and fulfilling. OK, maybe not quite so extreme, but once you've finished the process of writing the first book, the second one, and the ones following, *should* become easier.

You might already have a series mapped out in your head. Or you might think of further parts of the story even as you are finishing the first book. You might finish a trilogy, then think of something to go with it, like a prequel or a spin-off series.

On the other hand, some books are complete stories in themselves. They have a beginning, a middle, and an end, and they're done. Don't feel pressured to write a sequel if you don't want to.

WHAT ABOUT SHORT STORIES AND POEMS?

If you are an instant gratification sort of person, you might want to consider starting with poetry or short stories for your first submissions. You might even consider slice-of-life feel good stories (think *Chicken*

Soup for the Soul) or non-fiction articles for magazines. The great thing about these types of stories is they usually don't take as much time to write and you can send out several at a time (instead of waiting for months on one piece). It helps you become familiar with the process and it's a wonderful feeling when you get something published, no matter how short or small. Not to mention, publication of any kind looks good on your cover letter when you begin submitting to agents and editors.

Handy Definitions

Episodes: Short books that tell short stories with the same characters, in the same way a TV series has episodes.

Cliffhanger: A book that ends with unresolved plot lines. If you want to write books with intense endings but *no resolution,* we suggest having your series go up for sale all at once. *Pro:* The reader will usually quickly buy the next book in the series. *Con:* Many readers get irritated by this sort of sales 'gimmick' and might take out their frustrations in your reviews.

Sequel: A book that comes next in a series, continuing the same story that is already established.

Stand-alone: A book that can be read by itself without needing to read any other books, either before or after it in a series, to get the complete story.

Prequel: A book written about something that happened before the events of the series. (Think *The Hobbit* from *The Lord of the Rings,* or *Rogue One* from *Star Wars).*

Spinoff: Book(s) written about characters or events in a series separate from the original series.

QUESTIONS:

1. Are you a plotter, a pantser, or somewhere in between?
2. How long do you want your finished work to be?
3. If you're going to write a series, how many books do you want it to contain?

Chapter 5

CREATING LOVABLE CHARACTERS
(AND LOATHSOME)

"Often when you find your story or your MC (main character) isn't compelling enough, you can trace it back to the MC's passivity or reactivity in the story. Get your MC to make decisions and take actions that change the course of events, and boom! A much more effective protagonist and a better story."

— Rachelle Gardner, literary agent

Jamie's favorite aspect of any story is almost always its characters. She might not always remember their names, but she can recall the personality, attitude, and quirks of characters from movies she hasn't watched since childhood—and she can't even remember where she left her water bottle.

What is it, exactly, that makes a great character great? Why do we love them or hate them so much?

And—most importantly for writers—how does one go about creating such a thing?

We're not experts, and developing characters is definitely more of an art than a science, but there are a few guidelines we've discovered on our journey.

CHARACTERS ARE NOT HUMANS

"What?" you say. "Don't say that! I love him! And he loves me, too!"

We're sorry, but characters are very much not human. Sure, they may *act* like humans, but don't let them deceive you.

- **Humans are infinitely more complex than characters.** Characters need to be designed for a reader to get to know them in a very short amount of time. How long does it take to get to know a well-defined character? Maybe a few chapters. How long does it take to get to know a human? Years.

- **Characters are more predictable than humans.** A human will do what he or she does depending on their mood that day. Their actions can vary greatly depending on circumstances in their life, and yet still remain the same person.

  On the other hand, characters must be relatively predictable, or the reader will grow detached from them. Should they be *too* predictable? Definitely not, but they need to have a baseline that they generally hover around. Otherwise, your readers will feel like they don't know them.

- **Characters are more dramatic than humans.** OK, teenage girls might be the exception, but in general, characters need to be more dramatic than humans. Why? To express themselves, so the reader can get to know them.

This is especially true in the American culture today. If someone says something we disagree with, we are generally trained to just not say anything. But unless you can hear a character's thoughts to know their true feelings, they must express themselves in dialogue or action. Otherwise, the character is bland.

- **Never take a human and try to put them in a book... especially yourself.** This is a trademark of newbie writers, and yes, Jamie did make this mistake when she first started writing. It just doesn't work, because real people are too complex to translate into good characters.

However, some of your friends and family have awesome quirky traits that just *have* to make it into a character in your next book (I'm looking at you, Aunt Betsy). Feel free to take inspiration from people in your life when creating your own characters! Give your sidekick that funny accent or your villain that cowlick.

Just don't try to take Aunt Betsy in her full glory and cram her onto page ninety-two. Things could get messy.

LOVABLE CHARACTERS ARE FLAWED

Yes, you read that right. This is a controversial topic, because it's a common belief that people are generally good, but we subscribe to the idea that people aren't born inherently good. Watching a bunch of two-year-olds can substantiate this claim real quick.

Everyone has a weakness to some temptation... to some selfish habit. It could be anything: envy, pride, greed, lust, addiction—you name it. This is another way in which characters differ from humans: real people (starting with us) tend to struggle with nearly every issue at some point in their lives, but characters should only have one or two severe flaws that define them.

Resist the urge to make a perfect character. We're sorry, but perfect people do not exist, and making a perfect character simply won't be realistic. Your readers won't be able to really feel a connection with them.

Plus, dark secrets are just so juicy... why not use them to deepen your characters and reveal them as the story progresses? Readers love that stuff!

Just make sure the shadiness doesn't go deep enough to make your character unlikable. Readers might understand what your hero did in revenge after his father was killed, but they will never forgive him for killing a kitten.

MEMORABLE CHARACTERS HAVE QUIRKS

It could be a physical feature, a style of speech, a habit, an accessory... be creative! Recurring themes make characters more defined. Your characters' quirks will make your story come to life, help your readers form their own opinions about the character in question, and suck your readers deeper into the scene as they read.

Quirks can also be symbolic. Colors, stereotypes, and an animal-like tendency or look can all have a certain feeling associated with them, and attaching that feeling to your character will define them further.

Making a loathsome character? Give him or her an aspect that just makes you feel... uncomfortable.

RELATABLE CHARACTERS HAVE A WELL-DEVELOPED HISTORY

A character without a history is a missed opportunity to add depth to your story's world. You should know your character's heritage from the start to know why they act the way they do.

WHY DOESN'T YOUR CHARACTER LIKE
EGGS?

Because they remind him that he grew up in a poor household with nine siblings. The other children at school made fun of him for having an egg sandwich for lunch every day. And that rooster was evil… it chased him each morning when his mother sent him, grumbling and huffing, to fetch the dirty eggs from the hens' nests.

See what we did there? Even a little bit of history will go a long way to develop your character. Almost every reason why your character acts the way he or she does should be grounded in their own experiences.

MAIN CHARACTERS SHOULD GROW, BUT LOATHSOME CHARACTERS NEVER CHANGE

Emotionally, physically, spiritually, and mentally, all of your main characters should be on a path to change throughout the story, but not so much change that they become unrecognizable. Characters can change for the good and become more mature, stronger, happier... or they can spiral into darkness.

Loathsome characters, however, do not change. There is nothing attractive about stagnation. If you have an antagonist who you want to turn into a protagonist, they must change in order to get there. And during that process, they will become sympathetic to your reader. They might not become a full-fledged protagonist, but their change could be the catalyst for their transformation into an antihero.

Force your characters into situations they'd normally resist. Change can be painful, but pain is often necessary for positive results. Push, pull, and stretch your characters, and they will grow. If your character was comfortable enough to be able to sit around the house all day and eat potato chips, they wouldn't ever go on a death-defying adventure, and they wouldn't be very intriguing, would they?

WHERE TO START?

There isn't one cookie-cutter way to produce excellent characters, but here are some suggestions to get those cogs spinning.

Find characters you love and characters you hate from the latest movies, books, or TV shows, then ask *why* you feel that way. What is it about them that you find satisfying or distasteful? Are they fiery? Are they bland? Are they fun?

Nature

Research the 'four temperaments'—the ancient theory that there are four basic personality types—and start there for the 'nature' of your character. They are, in elementary terms: **choleric** (independent and decisive), **sanguine** (enthusiastic and social), **melancholic**(analytical and detail oriented), and **phlegmatic** (peaceful and artistic).

Also make sure you understand the differences in the genders. It may be controversial of us to say so, but males and females were designed with complementary differences. Can they have similar personalities? Sure! Can they fulfill non-stereotypical roles? Certainly!

But our hormones play a pivotal role in affecting how our brains function, and therefore how we interact with the world around us. Understanding this will make your characters of both genders more lovable and more realistic, especially if you're writing romance.

For example, a character with high testosterone levels (normally associated with males, but Jamie happens to be a female example) will tend to be more athletic. Whereas a character with high oxytocin levels will be more easily able to bond with other characters or creatures in your story. Check out the science—it's fascinating!

Of course there are exceptions to this rule, like Jamie. Understanding the science will allow you to better create realistic characters inside or outside the gender stereotypes.

Nurture

Build your character's complexity through their history and their environment. Your character should never be a certain way 'just because.'

In what type of environment and culture were they raised? What were their parents like? Did they have any siblings? What struggles did they encounter and overcome as they grew up? This will be the 'nurture' of your character.

PRACTICE MAKES PERFECT.

The best way to create anything is simply do it and learn through successes and failures. Pursue excellence, and over time you'll develop your own style. You can do it... now pick up a pen and write!

QUESTIONS:

1. Do your 'good' characters have flaws?
2. Do your 'bad' characters have realistic quirks?
3. How complex do you intend your side characters to be?
4. How can you make your characters more believable?

Chapter 6

PITFALLS TO AVOID
WHILE WRITING

"The road to hell is paved with adverbs."

— Stephen King

AVOIDING PITS LIKE INDIANA JONES

After reading this chapter's title you might be thinking, "Good grief, I barely have time *to* write and now these people are going to tell me what *not* to write?" Remember, we are trying to help you best utilize your time and spare you from pocketbook troubles—and future headaches—in the long run.

In our experience, these writing faux pas are the most widespread mistakes that a professional editor would tell you to weed out of your manuscript. Ignoring these pitfalls will make it more difficult for your manuscript to get accepted by an agent or editor.

If you plan to seek a traditional publisher, or if your intention is to go indie, you need to learn these concepts. Developing strong prose will help your writing shine, no matter where it ends up.

BUT WHYYYYYYYY?

You may read through some of these ideas and wonder why we recommend them. Maybe you've read best-selling authors that blithely ignore these 'rules.'

Consider this: top chefs put weird things in their dishes. Flavor combinations no one else would use. And their food tastes amazing... because they are experts and know what works together. So after you've been writing for a while, you will know when and how to 'break the rules.'

As you learn to work with these concepts, you will probably notice them more in the books you read. They begin to make more and more sense when you see how certain words and phrases can strengthen a concept or make it weaker.

Some of these ideas were put into place by writing trends which have phased out just as quickly (like sparkling vampires). But some people fail to realize that like shoulder pads, fads come and go, and editors want to see techniques that are relevant to the times.

This is not an exhaustive list of techniques, but these suggestions will get you started.

SWITCHING TENSE

One mistake many beginning writers make is to change tense from past to present to future willy-nilly. This can get extremely confusing. "She smiled up at him, then smacks him in the face with a sweet potato." Pick a tense and stick with it. Even when doing a flashback or memory section, that specific section should also stick to its own tense.

LONG OR INFO-DUMPING PROLOGUE

If you love fantasy or sci-fi, you might be thinking, "But I have to have a prologue! I have to explain the history of my world! I have to tell about the language and the clothing and the customs and why they somehow still celebrate Christmas!"

Of course, world building is crucial to these genres. But before you go dumping a bunch of information on your reader, give them a situation or a character they can care about. Then feed them little details about the land and customs throughout the story. The more invested readers become in a character, the more they will want to find out about your world.

This is called the 90% rule: despite all of your world building and research, only 10% of it should actually end up in your book. Otherwise, it will read like an encyclopedia. Instead of info-dumping, lace your descriptions and character interactions with details alongside a gripping scene—this is how we immerse the reader in a fascinating world without bogging them down.

Writers of epic fantasy have probably been developing their worlds in their heads for years, down to the tiniest ocean-blue leaf of the Havernashing Tree. If you write fantasy or sci-fi, it's important to write down the rules of your world (for example, whether magic is accessible to everyone or only certain chosen ones), regions, religions, type of environments, animals, level of civilization, et cetera. But blend it into your story little bits at a time, like seasonings in a dish.

Your prologue should serve one purpose before all else: to hook your new reader.

And remember, a large majority of readers skip right over prologues, anyway.

YAWN-INDUCING BEGINNING

We will touch on this in the editing chapters, but it's worth repeating and expanding upon, because the beginning of your book really is the most important part. Namely, the first page. And some would even argue the first *paragraph*.

Think about all the books you've read over the years from beginning to end. What about the books you didn't finish? What about the books you picked up and *never read past the first paragraph?*

Quite a few, right? Something just doesn't spark in that first paragraph and you decide to move on and find a book that might be more worth your time. This is especially important with Amazon Kindle books, where people can read the first few pages in a book for free.

Different genres will vary slightly when it comes to beginnings. For instance, young adult fiction will often begin with a bit of action, something to suck in young readers with short attention spans from the very first paragraph. Women's genres tend to start with the main character facing some sort of emotional challenge, like a difficult breakup or a new chapter of their lives.

Start your book with a snappy situation that captures the reader's interest and won't let it go. Thread your first chapter with tiny 'hooks' that keep yanking in the reader and make them want to know what happens next.

HEAD HOPPING

If you decide to write first person or third person, stick with that perspective. Only switch to a different perspective at a scene break or a new chapter.

Imagine that your reader is like a camera taped to the top of that character's head. They can only see, feel, taste, smell, and hear what that character can. We should be stuck inside their brain. And unless your MC can read minds, they won't know what other characters are thinking or feeling.

Here's an example:

Wrong:

> *Stacy leaned against the table. Her stomach growled and her mouth watered.*
> *Harold stood across from her. He wanted food too.*

Stacy is established as the point-of-view character when we feel her stomach growl and her mouth water. Therefore, we shouldn't know that

Harold wanted food too, unless he actually told Stacy, or he implied it from something she can discern.

Also wrong:

> *Stacy leaned against the table. Her stomach growled and her mouth watered.*
> *Harold stood across from her. "Wow, I'm really hungry," he thought.*

Unless Stacy is a mind-reader, she can't hear Harold's thoughts.

Right:

> *Stacy leaned against the table. Her stomach growled and her mouth watered.*
> *Harold stood across from her. He picked up the plate of cookies and smiled. "Wow, I'm hungry."*

Here we go! Everything Harold does is now perceivable only from Stacy's point of view. But we still get the idea just fine without breaking Stacy's POV, right?

It's fine to shift POV throughout a book, but we recommend you keep the sections separate and defined. Establish whose POV you are in as quickly as possible. Also, we don't recommend too many different POVs in a single book. Jamie's novels in *The Sentinel Trilogy* have three POVs each—and writing even that many can be nightmarish!

DIALOGUE TAGS AND ACTION TAGS

Decades ago, there was a trend to use creative dialogue tags in the place of 'said.' But this generally only distracts from the conversation. Instead of coming up with wild and random dialogue tags (conversed, heckled, babbled, bellowed, spluttered), it's generally best to use 'asked' or 'said.' We are not saying you should *never* use a different tag, just rarely.

However, you *can* and should use action tags instead of dialogue tags as much as possible. Consider the following:

Boring:

"How can you say that?" Shelly said. "I've loved you ever since I can remember."

Better:

"How can you say that?" Shelly clenched her fists and blinked in an unsuccessful attempt to keep tears from slipping down her cheeks. "I've loved you ever since I can remember!"

Dialogue tags carry a story along; they give dialogue a framework to dance around.

HE SAW, SHE KNEW

If you are writing from someone's POV, then everything you write will be something they saw or knew. So you can pretty much cut these words from your manuscript.

Example:

Wrong:

Justin walked into a room. He saw that all the fruitcake was gone from the dish on the counter.

Right:

Justin walked into a room. All the fruitcake was gone from the dish on the counter.

Wrong:

Mary went to the store, because she knew they were having a sale on strawberries.

Right:

Mary went to the store for the strawberry sale.

NOT ENOUGH DESCRIPTION

One of the challenges of writing is to pull the reader into your story. Make them a part of what's going on. Here are some things to look for and replace.

'She felt' can almost always be replaced with an emotional physical response. For example, instead of "She felt angry," try, "She clenched her teeth. Her heart slammed against her ribs. Her hands balled into fists and she paced up and down the hallway, stomping into the threadbare carpet."

Emotional physical responses are also great to convey facial expressions. For example, instead of "She had a worried look on her face," write "Her brow was furrowed, and her mouth pulled down at the corners."

Instead of using mundane descriptions, be specific. Instead of saying, "Her eyes were beautiful," describe *how* they were beautiful. "Sheryl's eyes were violet, with a perfect fringe of velvety lashes."

TOO MUCH DESCRIPTION

Like the info-dump prologue, many writers give a paragraph or longer description of a character right at the beginning of a story. There are ways to show what a character looks like in little bits, not all in one go. Find ways to show bits and parts of a character every time they talk in action tags or emotional physical responses (EPRs).

" I wrote on and off when my children were young, but I wasn't disciplined enough to really study the craft. I thought a good story was enough. It's not. It wasn't until my children were much older that I realized I had to study the craft the same way a musician studies an instrument. Practice and learn."

Beth Wiseman

Bestselling, award-winning author of over 30 novels and novellas

AVOID CLICHÉS

- Silent as a lamb.
- It might not be much, but it's home.
- It wasn't rocket science.
- Black as night
- Paper-thin

If you've heard a phrase a million times, try to think of a new way to describe it. Instead of "fragile as an egg shell," for example, you could say, "fragile as a dragonfly's wing." We know of thousands of thin things. Come up with something unique to your writing, but make sure it fits with the tone and character of your setting and/or main character. For example, a big, burly soldier might not think, "The hill unrolled before them, embellished with flowers like jewels on a rich lady's purse."

Also, don't overuse analogies and metaphors. If they come one after another, they lose the wow factor and distract from the story. Sprinkle them in like salt—enough to flavor, but not enough to overwhelm.

Another type of cliché to avoid would be repeating specific EPR's too often.

- He shrugged.
- She gasped.
- He smiled.
- Her heart pounded.

These are good in moderation, but you don't want the same descriptors on every page. Humans make thousands of physical gestures with all parts of their bodies. Get creative. Make faces in the mirror. Ask your children to make faces or act happy, sad, mad, etc. An awesome resource is *The Emotion Thesaurus* by Angela Ackerman. We both use this book every time we write.

AVOID CLICHÉ BEGINNINGS

We covered this in Chapter 3, but it bears repeating. Try to avoid cliché beginnings that will make readers roll their eyes and wonder if they've already read the book. (Angela's note: I've used a few of these. I deeply regret it, but what's done is done.)

- **The morning routine.** MC wakes up, gets ready for the day, eats breakfast, etc.
- **The daily grind.** The MC heads to school, work, spaceship, etc. and then introduces a cast of characters.
- **The chosen.** Dystopian trend of being selected for a job or given a preselected spouse or mate.
- **The pensive MC.** Character staring out a car, house, or plane window, pondering how they have been forced to move in with a relative, go to a new school or job, or move to a new state.
- **Everybody dies.** Chaos and death of every person an MC loves, and it all happens in the first page.
- **Mirror description.** MC looks in a mirror and gives a self-description, usually non-flattering.
- **The dream.** A dream sequence or waking up from a dream.
- **Smelling the roses.** Long description of a town or house with no main characters introduced. Yes, many great writers from the days of yore got by with this, but readers of the now want to know *who* they're reading about.
- **The unrelated.** Introduction of characters and/or concepts that have nothing to do with the rest of the story.
- **Detached dialogue.** Long stretches of dialogue without really knowing where the MC is or what's going on.

INTRODUCING TOO MANY CHARACTERS AT ONCE

This can especially happen in a sci-fi type of book where there's a team of people working together, or a friendship-type book where you have an MC who meets a group of friends at one time. Try to introduce characters one at a time, and give each one unique characteristics so the reader can remember who you are talking about. If you simply *must* introduce a group all at once, go with a few names and a few characteristics for a few people, and then filter in more details intermittently.

REPETITION

One of Angela's worst habits in writing is over-explaining. She will find herself writing the same thing over and over again in a different way, in case her readers didn't catch it the first time. Make sure you aren't over explaining a concept. Try to get the message across once, in an entertaining way, so your reader catches it the first time. Readers are pretty sharp!

AVOID OVERUSED WORDS

A few to watch out for: She was, they were, just, always, very, really, that, rather, literally, completely, quite, up, down, absolutely. Every writer has their own set of words they overuse—our friend Abigayle Claire *(Martin Hospitality)* says she tends to overuse 'well'. This is another reason why beta readers and editors are worth their salt: it's difficult for us writers to see our own repetition.

ADVERBS AND 'ING' WORDS (GERUNDS AND PARTICIPLES)

We are not militant about never, ever using adverbs, but they should be used sparingly (excuse us: in moderation). You can almost always strengthen a section of writing by replacing an adverb with a strong verb.

For example:

> *She moved down the street quickly.*

Could be:

> *She hurried down the street.*

Another example:

He walked shakily.

Could be:

His legs trembled with every step.

The same can be said of words that end with 'ing':

She was always drawing pictures while sitting on the porch.

Could be:

She always drew pictures when she sat on the porch.

You have to also be careful because sometimes sentences with 'ing' words don't make any sense.

Coasting down the street, Harold arrived at the green porch in no time.

Since Harold cannot be on the porch and the street at the same time, this sentence is poorly structured. Revise to:

Harold coasted down the street and arrived at the green porch.

Again, gerunds and participles have their place, just use them in moderation. We suggest limiting them to 1-2 per page. Of course, that doesn't always work. Try your best.

DON'T BE DISCOURAGED. KEEP GOING!

The great thing about a first draft is no one else has to see it (and no one probably *should* see it). You can spill out your thoughts with no regard for rules in the most haphazard way possible. So if these 'rules' drag you down into a swamp of "I can never write anything again" despair, then don't worry about them... for now. But please come back to this chapter for the second draft! Also, the more you write, the more these habits will flow naturally. It's like learning any new skill—it takes practice. The rough draft for your second book will probably be much smoother.

QUESTIONS:

1. Is my opening paragraph strong enough?
2. How can I make my opening chapter as strong as possible?
3. What writing habits do I need to break?

Chapter 7

CRITIQUE GROUPS
AND THE WRITERS' SORORITY

"The main thing I try to do is write as clearly as I can. I rewrite a good deal to make it clear."

— E.B. White, author of *Charlotte's Web*

So, you've written some stuff and you need guinea pigs.

What do you do? Call your mom and ask her to read your precious work? Cozy up to Aunt Suzie? Make your older kids read it?

Maybe... if any of those people actually enjoy reading your genre. Your family members may not be in your target audience.

And they might not be excited about your writing at all. This can be especially painful for writers—we've both gone through it—but you can't let it get under your skin. Don't expect every one of your family members to gobble up your book. From our experience, you'll be lucky if even one of them reads it (no matter what they promise). So set your expectations low and don't let it hurt you.

Besides potential damage to relationships, it's not a good idea to involve your family with your writing as a general rule. Why? Because they might say whatever they think you want to hear to encourage you, or they may avoid pointing out errors so as not to upset you. Also, they probably don't know the first thing about editing, or what's best for your manuscript. And your four-year-old will probably just want "more cats."

So where do you look for guinea pigs? Should you hire an editor as soon as your manuscript is complete?

No!

If this is your first writing project, we don't recommend hiring a professional editor right away. It takes years to develop good prose, and there are plenty of free (or cheap) options that can help you improve before you're ready for fine-tuning from a professional editor. Editors can be extremely expensive—if you hire one before you've got the essentials of good prose down, you'll end up paying for multiple rounds of pricey edits!

So, between Aunt Suzie and Professor Edits-a-lot, where should you hunt for guinea pigs?

CRITIQUE GROUPS (AND WHERE TO FIND THEM)

Grabbing critiques from other writers is one of the easiest—and most pocketbook-friendly—ways to refine your craft. Other writers need critiques just as much as you do, and most who are just starting out are willing to do a 'crit swap' with you.

- **Forums.** There are plenty of writing forums online. Good places to start your critiquing journey are writers groups in your specific genre—for example, the American Christian Fiction Writers (ACFW) group has many critique groups in the form of email lists. A membership cost may be associated with joining a group like this, but there are normally other perks associated with membership as well (like a discount on conference tickets or online resources).

- **Critique-oriented websites.** Also, there are several websites dedicated to fostering a good critiquing environment, like scribophile.com. You can join for free and post your work (in 3,000-word increments) for every five works from other people that you critique. This is a great place to find people you can trust to give good critiques and forge long-lasting friendships.

- **Facebook.** Facebook groups are excellent places for writing communities. Search for your genre and you're bound to find some starter options where writers swap critiques and reviews. And the more friends you make, the more likely you are to get invited to private groups that might have more advanced writers to further refine your craft.

Wherever you go for critiques, target writers who are more experienced than you, or people whom you feel you can trust. Beware of other writers who may try to change your style to become like theirs— protect your unique voice.

Make sure you understand what the other writer wants in terms of feedback. They may be looking for overall impressions or a 'pat on the back.' You don't want to spend countless hours meticulously line-critiquing to receive back: "I liked your writing a lot. Good job."

On that note, make sure you always give an equal swap—critique their first ten pages in exchange for your first ten pages. Don't ask them to critique your novella in exchange for their 130,000 word sci-fi space opera.

And be careful not to bite off more than you can chew! It's easy to get swamped with critiques and run out of time for your own writing. We've learned that one the hard way.

A NOTE ON CHILDREN'S BOOKS

The awesome thing about children's books is you have a built-in target audience under your roof! Do try reading your picture book drafts and middle grade chapter books to your children. They will give you great feedback for what works and what doesn't. Watch their reactions. Are they paying attention while you read? Do they remember key details at the end of the story? Pass your manuscripts on to friends with children of similar age and ask them to check out your stories. Adult critique groups are still useful for picture books and middle grade books, but your best feedback will come from your target audience.

THE CHEERLEADER AND THE GRINCH

Everyone loves a cheerleader. Kids make great little encouragers, especially if a cookie bribe is involved. But if you manage to get a bunch of friends and family to read your books, they are most likely going to tell you what they think you want to hear, even if it means bending the truth a little bit.

So go ahead and pass out manuscripts to your eagerly waiting fans. Bask in the praise for a moment. And then go find some complete strangers and ask their opinions.

Even though most people will gush over your work, you may also encounter a few grinches. Great Aunt Maribelle, for instance, might think your dystopian fantasy is 'too dark,' while Uncle Harold might simply declare steampunk is a 'stupid concept.' Just remember, not everyone will like the genre you write. And your two-year-old may inexplicably and simply say, "bananas." Not everyone likes the same style of music, not everyone likes the same type of food. It's fine.

Plus... if you need to put this book down for a moment to get some Nutella and graham crackers for comfort, we will understand... *not everyone is going to want to read your book.* This can be a hard pill to swallow. But some people don't really like to read—gasp!—and some might not have time. As a mom, we're sure you have to be choosy about what you read, since you don't have time to read everything. (Angela only has time to read in the bathtub usually, and she's found she can only stay in there so long). So don't let it get you down if someone doesn't get around to reading your work. There are plenty of people out there who will love your writing—and we will help you find them.

Superfans are good, but don't let it get to your head. Yes, there will be these wonderful, amazing people in your life who absolutely love everything you write and demand more after they've devoured every page. If you ask for feedback, they will clasp their hands in rapture and say, "It was all simply wonderful!"

These types of fans are crucial to writers, since of course we want people to like our books and buy every one of them, right? But people who absolutely love your work will love it so much they won't see the flaws—the glaring issues that stick out to the majority of readers.

However, those wonderful, fawning emails and Amazon reviews are certainly nice to pull out and read when you're trying to write your tenth chapter of the third novel in a series at 11:30 at night and your baby wakes up. Again.

THE WRITERS' SORORITY: ALPHA AND BETA READERS

If you want to make a career out of writing, your most valuable asset over time will be what's called a 'street team'—the people who love your books and support your writing over the course of your career. It could be your first five fans if you're starting out, or it could be fifty or a hundred or more as you gather a team over time. Yes, you can get there!

Don't be intimidated—it normally takes at least a year to build up a street team and find good alpha and beta readers. If you're reading this book, you're probably just starting out, and we're not trying to burden you or make you think you should have dozens of people wanting to critique your work already. You probably don't, and that's fine! But if you can build a support network early, the benefits will be well worth the investment.

Street teams are invaluable for marketing purposes and making sure you get reviews on your book's launch day. They are normally collected with your email newsletter list or a Facebook group, but for now we'll focus on their value as critiquers. (We'll talk more about your street team and email newsletter list in both *The Busy Mom's Guide to Indie Publishing* and *The Busy Mom's Guide to Novel Marketing.*)

To start your street team, first, you'll want to find people whom you trust who might not be professional editors, but great at critiquing and really share your vision and love for your books. They don't pull any punches, but they know how to spot your strengths and encourage you as well.

Jamie calls these people 'alpha' readers, because they get the first look at your rough draft before anyone else. They might read behind you as you write, gobbling up each chapter as you finish it and letting you know any major flaws they find before they could affect your whole book (plot holes... *shudder*). Jamie only has three alpha readers, and she snuggles them tight and listens closely to their suggestions.

When your manuscript is complete, it goes to a larger portion of your street team—the 'beta' readers. Beta readers might not be awesome critiquers or know how to spell supercalifragilisticexpialidocious, but their feedback can still be really valuable. The more eyes on your manuscript, the better likelihood of typos or continuity errors being spotted. Jamie opens applications for each book's beta team to her email newsletter list and selects around fifteen applicants per project.

Then, after professional editing, the rest of your street team—and anyone you select—gets one of your ARCs (Advance Reader Copies). This is an almost-final version of the book that's printed (or formatted into an ebook) to catch last-minute errors that snuck through the editing process. ARC readers help weed out any remaining issues, and hopefully leave reviews for your book on launch day.

To develop your team, write consistently and be on the look-out for critiquers as you write. Make friends at your local library, with people at your mom's night or church or running team. Introduce yourself at book

One of Jamie's alpha readers, R.J. Metcalf, loved Jamie's books but didn't think she could start writing while raising two young boys. After a year of chatting, critiquing, and encouraging each other online, they met in person at a writer's conference. Now that R.J. has decided to start writing her own books, they are each other's alpha readers, attend events together every year, and chat frequently online about their crazy kiddos.

clubs and Facebook groups and book blog—not in a pushy or creepy way, but to genuinely make friends. Be awesome to people and you'll probably get some awesomeness back!

NO MATTER WHAT

No matter what kind of feedback you get, helpful or unhelpful, the very best response is a "Thank you." You can cry and grumble and go kick your kid's Elmo doll (while the kids are at grandma's, of course) as much as you need to in the privacy of your own home. But for the people who have taken the time and effort to read your work and provide feedback, you need to say thank you. If you feel like they misread something and you need to clarify, that's fine, but be polite about it. Read your response out loud and listen for your tone. Make sure there are no undertones of irritation. This is very important.

Why? After you have gone through the emotional turmoil of seeing so many red and highlighted lines and start really reading the suggestions, you might realize your critiquer has taught you some invaluable writing skills you will implement the rest of your life. We have both experienced this multiple times.

If you receive feedback you find completely unhelpful, still say, "Thank you so much for your time." Then throw it out and don't ask that person for help again. It's as simple as that.

CONFERENCES: WORTH IT?

Conferences, workshops, and writing retreats can cost a pretty penny for anyone when factoring in the registration price, airfare, lodging, and food, and as busy moms, the price for time away from our family might be even higher. But if you can manage to escape your toddler's spaghetti-sauce-laden fingers for few days, a time to focus on writing—and a mental break—may be worth every cent.

Jamie tries to attend one to three conferences each year, depending on the availability of childcare and, of course, the ability to budget for them. Bear in mind that the cost of a conference doesn't necessarily dictate how valuable it will be to you, and that many conferences offer scholarships.

Perhaps the greatest value of a conference, in our opinion—aside from the classes and networking—is the opportunity to have your writing critiqued by successful authors, editors, or agents associated with the conference.

Yes, you heard that right.

Whatever level you consider your writing to be, most conferences will allow you to submit your first ten pages or so to a professional for their critique. You can use your first ten pages of any project. We recommend bringing in the manuscript that needs the most polishing and strongest hooks to snag your readers. Normally the cost for this is only $30-$50.

Don't be scared! Jamie orders a critique at every conference she attends with this option. The more advice we can get from pros, the better—and that price is extremely cheap compared to most professional editors! It also allows you to network with a star for a possible mentorship from a successful author, a chance to see if you groove with an editor before hiring them, or to give an agent a taste of what you have to offer.

To find a conference that's right for you, target an event that's specifically for your genre. If it's right up your alley, you'll have a better chance of hearing advice that's perfect for your writing and making long-lasting, priceless friendships.

Finding good critiquers and building relationships—and a street team with great alpha and beta readers—can take years. But if you're in this for the long haul, those relationships will prove priceless to your career.

QUESTIONS:

1. Would I do better with an online critique group or a local writer's group?
2. Is a writer's conference something I could budget time and money for right away?
3. How am I going to handle critical feedback?

Chapter 8

THE DREADED RED INK:
EDITING

> *"Writing a book is a horrible, exhausting struggle, like a long bout of some painful illness. One would never undertake such a thing if one were not driven on by some demon whom one can neither resist nor understand."*
>
> — George Orwell, author of *Animal Farm*

We hope you've saved this chapter until after you've worked on your writing project for awhile already. You've read the last chapter about critiquing, right? You don't want to hire an editor too soon and waste money. As busy moms, we want to save as much moolah as possible. Mommy's sippy cup needs refills.

Or perhaps you're thumbing ahead in the book, since you've already been through your story three times and can't find any more grammatical errors. Your manuscript is printed in black rows, crisply sheeted. Or saved in a file, ready to be attached to a cover letter. So it must be ready, right?

Not if it hasn't been professionally edited. Please don't submit it anywhere yet.

We have said this in an earlier chapter, but we'll say it again in case someone skipped ahead. (Not that *you* would ever do that, right? Eh, we all do it).

Maybe you're thinking, "My book might be a little imperfect, but the plotline is great."

Editors at publishing houses rarely glance over a poorly-edited first draft and say, "Ooh, what a great story idea! We'll whip this right into shape."

Nope, nope, nope. You are trying to get noticed out of thousands of manuscripts, remember? If writing is riddled with rookie mistakes—issues such as lengthy prologues, head hopping, or POV violations—you can guarantee that manuscript will be going straight to a reject pile.

And if you self-publish, you will probably publish with Amazon. With both paperback and Kindle services, they offer what is called a preview, which means potential buyers of a book can read the first few pages before they spend a penny. While some readers are willing to overlook a few typos for the sake of a good story, several mistakes per chapter will definitely cut down your sales numbers. You want to make sure your first few pages are as exciting and genre-appropriate as possible, because they are vital to selling your book.

BUT REALIZE...

No matter how much you pay for editing, or how many eyeballs scan through your pages, you are going to miss a comma, or repeat a word, or something. Most best-sellers out there have typos, and once you start looking for them you'll see them pop up everywhere.

Of course, this doesn't mean we don't strive for the best product possible. There's a big difference between one misplaced comma and an error on every other page of a book.

Also realize that you won't notice your own mistakes most of the time (especially if you're just starting out in your writing journey). Our brains do this really awesome thing where they automatically fix problems as we read, like filling in missing letters in familiar words.

OK, maybe it's not so awesome from an editing perspective. But a professional editor can hone in on issues like moms can sniff out poopy diapers.

BEFORE YOU HIRE AN EDITOR

We've discussed this before, but for the skimmers, we'll say it again. Run your story through a good critique group before you even think about editing.

A good critique group can be as helpful, in some opinions (including Angela's), as a college class on creative writing. And we don't mean some forum filled with excitable girls writing fan fiction, even though there is nothing wrong with that. We mean people who will read your work, say what they like about it, then chop up the rest and serve it back to you in tiny, red-lined bits.

Editors for big time publishing companies do not make money by being nice. And we can guarantee you that Amazon reviewers who are complete strangers can be downright brutal.

Don't believe us? Check out some of the reviews on books by your favorite authors. You can't avoid all negative reviews, but having good editing will cut down on the grammar trolls dramatically. Less trolls equals higher ratings, which equals more sales in your pocket.

"My first indie book project was funded by my husband... I was a magazine editor, so I had contacts who became my friends. A good friend edited my book, another good friend laid it out... It felt as if everyone was so supportive, everyone wanted to help me get this book out. It was wonderful.**"**

Ines Bautista-Yao

Author of *Only A Kiss*

HOW MANY DRAFTS?

Every writer is going to have a different number of drafts they put their story through before they feel like it's ready, and it might even be different for every book they write. Angela does two drafts on her own, a third and fourth (sometimes a fifth) with a critique group, and then a sixth final polish after beta reading.

Jamie lets her alpha reader team and critiquers shred her first and second drafts, then lets her editor(s) and beta reader team loose on the third draft. Draft four is for her proofer, and the final draft is her own proofing run once the book is in its final format. This is one luxury of indie publishing: you can weed out missed errors after your book is already published. But it's still a pain in the neck (and extra formatting costs can be expensive), so make your book as perfect as possible for its launch.

If you come to a point where you are sick and tired of looking at your book, you might need a bit of time between edits. Give yourself a few days or even a month, write a short story or even a personal letter. Or just binge-watch *Friends* reruns; we won't judge. Then come back with a fresh perspective. It helps more than you'd think.

CONSIDER PAYING FOR A MINI EDIT

We already covered this in Chapter 7. Jamie swears by 'mini edits,' which can be 10-page edits, your first 2,000 words, or something around that length.

Jamie pays for one at every conference she attends, from bestselling authors or agents or editors. Conferences tend to give great discounts on these, so expect to pay around $30-$50, which is much cheaper than a full editing service. And worth every penny.

An added bonus is that your first 10 pages are what need the most editing, anyway—that's where your strongest hooks must be developed. The better your hooks, the more likely your reader will read your book through to the end. And then buy the next book in the series.

TYPES OF EDITORS

There are several different types of editors, and each come with their own expertise and set of costs. Here are a few of the types:

- **Developmental/Substantive.** This is the type of editor who will help you figure out that snappy first line, tell you your character is not interesting enough or let you know if you should trash the whole chapter. This is a framework editor that helps you build the best foundation for your story.

  Arguably, this can also be accomplished by alpha and beta readers and a critique group. Developmental editors can be extremely helpful for new writers, but they can also be expensive.

  Also consider that if you hire a developmental editor, you will still have only one person's feedback. It often helps to have several pairs of eyes because people often focus on 'pet' issues and miss other problems.

  Consider a cooking contest with three judges. Each judge might have a subjective opinion and taste. One might focus on flavor above all, while another focuses on texture, and a third considers presentation above everything else. All three are needed to make a well-rounded judgment.

  It's normal for new writers to need several rounds of developmental edits on the same manuscript. It's a learning process, which is why we recommend starting with critique groups, so you might avoid having to pay for a round or two of professional developmental edits.

- **Copy editor/Line editor.** No matter how meticulous you are with grammar, you are going to miss a few things—

especially when you've been working so close with a story. (And if your child has decided not to sleep again until their tenth birthday). We recommend you hire a copy editor as the second to last step before formatting your indie book or sending off your manuscript to a traditional publisher or agent.

If you can find a few friends who are great with SPAG (spelling, punctuation and grammar), all the better. Angela has three people copy edit her final manuscript (two are professionals) and there's always one or two mistakes each person will find that the other two don't spot.

- **Proofreader.** Proofers are your last line of defense against typos. Often times, new errors can crop up when you're fixing old ones. And, yeah, even professionals make mistakes. So it helps to have a proofer read the fully edited manuscript for the first time, with fresh eagle eyes.

  This service tends to be cheaper than line editing, but many professionals will not proof a book unless it has already gone through developmental and line edits.

- **Acquisition Editor.** This person will be your go-between if your manuscript is chosen by a traditional publishing company. They will tell you to make edits—and sometimes massive re-writes— to better suit the publisher's desires, not to help you learn how to write. They expect you to be a seasoned writer, and generally won't hold your hand like an independent editor would.

HOW TO CHOOSE YOUR EDITOR

Please don't Google editors and pick the first one that pops up.

Research them!

So many times we've contacted other indie authors to let them know about glaring errors, and they will write back, "We paid two thousand dollars to have our book professionally edited!"

- **Choose an editor who has experience with your genre.** Editors of specific genres will know what your readers are looking for, and will help you catch issues that might affect their enjoyment of your work.

- **Always ask for samples.** Most editors will go through a certain numbers of pages for a small price to show you how they will edit the rest of your piece.

- **Check out the editor's portfolio.** Look up the titles they've edited on Amazon and check out their reviews. Are there a lot of complaints about editing issues? (Ignore the trolls.)

- **Ask other authors for recommendations.**

- **Make sure your editor is familiar with your country of origins alternative spelling and idioms.** Australia, England, the US, and Canada (along with many other English-speaking countries) have their own little quirks in spellings and sayings, and if you are pitching to an editor in your own country they will be expecting you to keep things local. So if you're Australian but hiring an editor from the USA, for example, make sure they will be able to meet your country-specific needs.

- **Consider turn-around time.** An editor should be able to give you a general date they will have a manuscript ready by. Always add a few weeks to this date in case of personal situations.

EXPECT TO PAY A FAIR WAGE

Hiring an editor is like hiring a mechanic; you get what you pay for. Don't go cheap, but do compare prices. Most editors will have their prices outlined on their website or Facebook page. Make sure you always get a quote upfront so you know what to expect.

Editing can cost you anywhere from $50 to $3,000+, depending on what type of editing you want, how many rounds of editing you need, and the editor you select. Here are the ranges we've encountered (beware editors who ask for more):

- **Developmental/Substantive:** $100-$700
- **Copy/Line:** $150-$2,000
- **Proofing:** $50-$500

Check out Chapter 10: The Next Steps for more details regarding the costs of producing your book.

QUESTIONS:

1. How many rounds of edits do you think your favorite book went through?
2. How much are you willing to spend on editing? Is it worth saving up for?
3. How does it make you feel when you see multiple typos in a book you are reading?

Chapter 9

INDIE, TRADITIONAL, OR HYBRID?
GESUNDHEIT.

> *"If a nation loses its storytellers, it loses its childhood."*
>
> — Peter Handke

If you are just stepping into this world of writing, you might be confused when asked what type of writer you are. A writer's a writer, right? (Oops, lapsing into Dr. Seuss-esque verse here. We'd better slow down before we start craving green eggs and ham).

We discussed how to pinpoint what you want to write. In this chapter we will address writing for profit. So if your first goal is to have time to write letters or a baby book or something simply to share and not to make money, you don't have to read this chapter. You can frolic ahead and write those scrapbook pages.

But if you're dreaming of the day when you can go to Amazon, type your name in the search bar and see the cover of your book, you'll have to decide what method of publishing you want to go with.

THEN AND NOW

In the years of yore, when there was no internet and no Amazon and no Kindle books, most new authors had two options. They could send their manuscripts to traditional publishers and hope and pray to get a book deal, or they could scrape up money and pay a company to publish their book for them.

Because of the time and effort to get a traditional publisher, companies called vanity presses sprang out of the woodwork. Some of these companies were there to legitimately help authors by giving them a reasonable, affordable way to produce their work. But many used flattery to scam authors out of hundreds or thousand of dollars. More often than not, authors would wind up with a garage filled with poorly edited, poorly produced books, and only a few family members would purchase them.

Then along came ebooks and Amazon, which changed the self-publishing game forever. Amazon's Kindle platform provides a way for anyone to publish their book for free, in an instant. Amazon provides a billion potential customers and a worldwide platform, as opposed to the olden days, when self-published authors had to rely on word of mouth and book signings to sell their darlings.

AMAZON KINDLE: THIS IS A GOOD AND BAD THING

Why could this be a bad thing, you might wonder. We mean, you don't have to wait months for a publisher to *maybe* pick your manuscript out of a slush pile of thousands. And you don't have to pay a vanity press thousands of dollars, either.

Consider this. If anyone can publish a book... *anyone* can publish a book.

Amazon doesn't have a team of a thousand people reading through every manuscript that gets published to check for errors and plot holes. So the majority of material thrown up on Amazon probably didn't go through the refining fire it needed to, and thus the stigma of all independent books being terrible was born.

But that stigma is fading over time as independent books like *The Martian* and *Wool* are becoming bestsellers and being made into movies. There are definitely good indie books out there, and yours could join their ranks if you put the time, effort, and money into making it professional.

REACHING FOR THE TRADITIONAL DREAM

Every writer dreams of moment when you receive that letter in the mail, tear it open and read those blessed words: "Dear Writer, we have read your manuscript and were so profoundly moved that we all went out for cake. Enclosed you will find your contract and a check for one hundred thousand dollars."

Well, most of us know publishing contracts might be just a bit more back and forth than that, but nevertheless, that's what every writer should strive for, right? Well... maybe.

PROS OF GOING TRADITIONAL

- **Gratification of being chosen from hundreds, maybe thousands of other writers.** Let's face it, it's an *American Idol* moment. You get the golden ticket. You win. And if you're *really* blessed, you might even get picked by one of the Big Five publishers. The odds are stacked *high* against you, but it could happen.

- **Advance payment.** Depending on the size of the publishing company—and the genre of your book—you could receive several thousand dollars in what's known as an advance, after the contract is signed and before any books are sold. Or it could be hundreds of dollars, or it could be nothing. Advances are not happening as much as they used to, especially for first-time authors.

- **A team of professionals working to make your book a success.** Traditional authors don't have to worry about hiring an editor, a cover designer, or a formatter—all of those details are handled by the publisher. They will also help with marketing around the time of your book's launch. (With most traditional publishers nowadays, you will still be expected to do a large portion of the marketing.)

- **Paperback distribution.** Many publishing companies have a sizable distribution market of bookstores all across the United States and even the world, which means your book will possibly appear on more shelves to be noticed by the adoring public.

And those bookstores in the distribution ring? Many authors don't realize that if their books don't sell within a few months, in some cases, their books are pulled off the shelves, sent back to the distributor, and *pulped*. Yes, this is true—ask any bookstore owner. It makes us sick to our stomachs just thinking about it. *Put on superhero capes and masks and run into the store like crazy people.* "Books, we've come to save you!"

REALITY CHECK: ADVANCES

Advances aren't just free money. They're an 'advance' on your royalties that your book is expected to make. Your publisher wagers that your book will perform well enough to make all of that money back, and then some. And if it doesn't earn out, that publisher probably isn't going to renew your contract. Not only that, but the advance has to be paid out before you see any extra royalties.

Here's an example of how it could go:

- You are offered a $5,000.00 advance.
- You will make 10% royalty on each book sold (actual royalty varies).
- The books sell for $15.00 each, so your royalty would be $1.50 per book.

Therefore, 3,333 books will have to be sold before your advance is paid off and you start receiving any kind of royalty check.

For more information about this subject, check out this very helpful and thorough article from *The Balance* (link in the Sources section).

If you're feeling like your six-year-old on the first day she went to ballet class and realized she didn't get to wear toe shoes yet, you're not alone. Most beginning writers have a starry-eyed idea of the fame and fortune writing might bring. But just because it's *rare*,doesn't mean it can't happen.

Please don't think we are trying to discourage you from putting your work out there. We want you to succeed. You *can* succeed. We're going to give you the tools have the best chance possible.

But whichever route you choose, traditional or indie, the truth remains the same. It's a *lot* of work. And it takes a *lot* of time, blood, sweat, and tears.

I'VE BEEN TRYING TO LAND A TRADITIONAL CONTRACT FOR MONTHS. WHY DOES MY WORK KEEP GETTING REJECTED?

Here are some things to consider if you've sent your work off to publishers or agents before and been rejected.

- **Presentation:** Have you studied the company's submission guidelines? Every publisher has slightly different manuscript presentation preferences. If you submit something that's not exactly what they've asked for, they will assume you didn't do your homework. Your proposal will end up in the trash without them even glancing at your writing. Remember—large publishers receive hundreds or thousands of proposals every day. They are looking for any excuse to reduce their slush pile.

   Maybe your query letter or proposal could use a facelift. Ask your critique group what they think of it, or consider hiring an editor or marketing specialist to edit it for you.

- **Genre and subject:** There is no point submitting a zombie story to a company that only publishes sweet westerns. But another angle to consider is the company that is inundated with the same kind of story. For instance, they might receive a fantastic idea for a coming of age story about a girl who befriends Clara Barton... but in the same stack might be a very similar story about the same historical character. They might decide to reject both stories simply to avoid a copyright lawsuit. *This happens every day.*

- **Quality:** So many writers send off their stories thinking, "Oh, I've got a great idea. The editor will love it. So what if it has some grammatical errors. That's what editors are *for,* right?"

Wrong. Editors are expecting a professional, error-free manuscript—this is one way to rise above the competition.

Consider this: If someone comes to a talent show and sings a Grammy award-winning song, but they're off key, they aren't going to win the talent show based on their song choice. Your manuscript needs to be as perfect as possible.

- **Quantity:** Unless you are extremely fortunate and have made some sort of outside connections, your little story-child, whom you've dressed in Sunday best with polished shoes and brand-new hair bows, will be dropped into what's called a slush pile.

The slush pile is the stack of submissions most editors receive on a daily basis. Many editors don't even go through these submissions themselves; they have assistants who sort through the bulk of the slush, pick out a few ideas they think might be interesting, and then throw out the rest. So there may be a number of 'gatekeepers' to work through before your precious story-child even gets a chance to smile up at the editor-in-chief of a fancy publishing company.

If the publisher you're targeting has a slush pile the size of

Mount Everest, maybe try putting some of your eggs in other baskets. Or submit at a different time. The one time of year you definitely *don't* want to submit in is after NaNoWriMo in November (National Novel Writing Month). Editors loathe this period because they are inundated with unedited manuscripts that newbies threw together as fast as possible to score Internet points.

- **Clichés:** Editors (and their minions) read dozens, maybe even hundreds of submissions every day. And there are trite manuscript openings that they see over and over again. We aren't saying that it's impossible to create an innovative, exciting story with these elements included. A talented, seasoned writer can make any story interesting. But if you want a chance with a traditional publisher, you might want to study up on clichés, which can also vary by genre. (Angsty teen moving to rainy small town in Washington, anyone?)

PROS OF GOING INDIE (SELF PUBLISHING)

- **You can write what you want, whenever you want, without anyone else telling you how to write it.** This is great, especially if you have a niche story that's hard to find an agent for. When Angela looked for an agent for her Christian middle grade fantasy sci-fi dystopian story, she found exactly one agent in the United States that would even look at a story in that genre. That's what eventually made her decide to go indie. Jamie had a similar experience with her clean urban fantasy young adult apocalyptic dystopian series (say that five times fast).

However, just because you have total writing freedom doesn't mean you can sneeze on the page and expect your book to sell.

You still have accountability to your audience to write something excellent—it just doesn't have to fit into a publisher's box.

- **You get to choose your own book cover designer and editor.** Traditional publishers would dictate these for you, and although you would probably still have a say, their opinion is final. But indie authors get to select their own cover artist and editor(s). Yes, you have to pay them from your own pocket, but you get to choose if you want a $5 cover or a $2,000 masterpiece. You get to talk directly with these people and tell them exactly what you want, so you have the most control.

- **You can produce books at the speed you wish to go.** If you want to take ten years to write an epic fantasy trilogy, it's fine. No editor is breathing down your neck to hurry up and get it finished. If you want to slam out six short novellas in a year to keep momentum and sales going (more on that later), you can. And you won't have to wait for a minimum of six months for each book to be completed and for the publisher to get everything together. The traditional publishing process can sometimes take years.

- **You get to keep all the profits.** When you self-publish, your platform (such as Amazon KDP for Kindle or CreateSpace for paperback) will keep a small cut for their role in distribution, but after that, it's all yours. And depending on what you publish and how you publish, that can add up to a tidy amount over the years in your career.

We can't tell you how many traditionally published authors (including bestsellers) we've talked to who barely make a big enough royalty check per month to buy a nice dinner. Yes, the advance might be nice, but a writer might never see more than a few dollars afterward (and nothing if their advance doesn't earn out). For some, the advance becomes a ball and chain. They feel forced into signing the next contract for financial reasons, then spend the next year or two struggling to meet the publisher's deadlines. Rinse and repeat.

You might find this hard to believe, but it's unfortunately true. This is why more and more big-name authors are becoming hybrid authors.

WAIT, WHAT? WHAT'S A HYBRID AUTHOR?

A hybrid author is someone who is both traditionally and independently published. Normally this happens when an established traditional author realizes they can make more money by indie publishing because they already have a loyal audience ready to buy their next book, regardless of who publishes it.

But smart agents and publishers realize that a successful indie author is a better investment than a debut author who doesn't know the ropes of the industry. It's a growing concern that some publishers are only interested in authors who already have established marketing platforms. This includes the size of your email newsletter list, your social media audience, and the visitors to your website.

Of course, this isn't always true—people's opinions vary. So if you're targeting a specific agent or publisher, ask them how they feel about working with an indie author (and show them your sales numbers, Amazon reviews, and the size of your social media or newsletter subscribers). If you can't get in touch online, consider attending a conference to get an appointment with them.

AREN'T INDIES JUST BAD WRITERS WHO CAN'T GET THEIR WORK PUBLISHED ANY-WHERE ELSE?

Ahem. No.

If you choose the indie route, you may hear this. From other writers, from relatives, or from people who come up to your book table, flip your book over, wrinkle their noses and ask, "So, which publisher are you with?"

This stigma came with the olden days we talked about before, where writers who couldn't get published with a traditional company would pay tons of money to a vanity press. It sticks because everybody's Aunt Suzie thinks her unedited memoir with a cover she designed in Microsoft Paint will put Stephen King to shame.

But something happened when Amazon started making a platform for self-published writers (called 'KDP' for Kindle Direct Publishing). Writers began to realize they could put together a book of their own creation. They wouldn't have to worry about their books being dictated by a big publishing company's editor, meeting stringent deadlines, and giving the majority of their royalties to a publisher.

At the time of writing this, neither Angela nor Jamie have signed a contract with a traditional publisher (though Angela's poetry and short stories have been published in traditional magazines, and Jamie has been pursued by several publishers and agents). Why? Well... if you make the investment, indie publishing has pretty sweet perks of its own.

I STILL CAN'T DECIDE HOW TO PUBLISH...

Don't stress. This is a big decision. Give it time.

Ask people in your critique group their opinions, research writing forums online, chat with your local bookstore owner, and get a babysitter so you can attend a local writers' event. The more first-hand experiences you hear, the more confident you will feel in making one decision or another.

And if you need more specifics on the details of indie publishing, check out the next book in this series, *The Busy Mom's Guide to Indie Publishing*. In it we address all of the most common concerns and questions about going indie, and we lay out detailed instructions for giving your book the best chance of success.

QUESTIONS:

1. Are any of my favorite authors independently published, or hybrid? Does that affect how I enjoy their writing?
2. Where can I find people with experience in the book industry who can give me advice on traditional publishing versus self publishing?
3. What effects would a traditional contract and deadlines have on my family? What about an indie career, where I would act as both the publisher and the author?

Chapter 10
THE NEXT STEPS

> "*We are all apprentices in a craft where no one ever becomes a master.*"
>
> — Ernest Hemingway

If you have made it to this chapter and feel encouraged and ready to fill up a notebook or type like crazy, we are so excited for you! We hope that you write oodles of wonderful things and that we've helped you on your journey. You are also passing on to your children the example of pursuing their own dreams, and creating books they might even want to read someday.

I HAVE THIS STUFF I WROTE. WHAT DO I DO NOW?

We'll go over a very short summary of where to go next with your awesome writing. However, the bulk of our advice for publishing and marketing can be found in the next two books in this series: *The Busy Mom's Guide to Indie Publishing* and *The Busy Mom's Guide to Novel*

Marketing.

When you've decided to go indie or pursue a traditional contract, and your manuscript is polished and shiny, you're finally ready to share it with the world. Will it ever be perfect? No. Years later, you will probably flip through your book and find things you wish you could change. But most artists have that problem, including us. The important thing is making sure your manuscript is something you are proud of.

A LIGHT DUSTING FOR TRADITIONAL SUBMITTERS

If you are going the traditional publishing route, we highly recommend that you purchase *A Writer's Market* (they also have versions for poets, short story writers, and children's authors). This is an annual resource book released by Writer's Digest around June each year. You can also get a monthly subscription to the service at writersdigestshop.com.

Also consider a temporary subscription to Publisher's Marketplace, a website that catalogs book deals between publishers and literary agents. Here you can find publishers who are currently buying books similar to yours. And you can see exactly how active and successful different literary agents are, and how much they're paying for book contracts. Check it out at publishersmarketplace.com.

Here are a few submission tips:

DECIDE IF YOU WANT TO FIND A LITERARY AGENT OR JUST SUBMIT DIRECTLY TO A PUBLISHER.

An agent is an extra step and cost, but they will do the hard work of matching your manuscript with the best publishing house. They can also help you find legal representation, open international and movie deal doors for you, and can become a priceless coach for your writing career.

An agent will present you and your manuscript in the best possible way to a publisher, perhaps even getting you through that first door without having to make it through the slush-pile round.

All of the largest publishers require you to have an agent before you submit to them. 'Unsolicited' manuscripts, or manuscripts from authors who aren't represented by an agent, are thrown straight in the trash. So if you don't get an agent, make sure you don't submit to those publishers. It's a waste of time.

An agent should *never* ask for money up front. They get paid when you get paid—about 12%-15% of your royalties on your book contracts they sign. So they truly have your best interest—and your book's success—at heart.

STUDY UP ON HOW TO CRAFT AN EXCELLENT QUERY LETTER/PROPOSAL.

Different genres and types of publishers will have different requirements for submissions. Some want a simple cover letter with three chapters, for instance. Some completely depend on a query.

Query Shark at queryshark.blogspot.com is an excellent resource for learning how to craft a query. Agent Query at agentquery.com is another great source that breaks down the components of a query letter and helps you get started on a search for an agent.

MAKE SURE YOUR SUBMISSION IS FORMATTED *EXACTLY* HOW THE PUBLISHER WANTS IT.

Don't just make multiple copies and send them all out. Some publishers prefer specific fonts and styles. The first step through the door is to show them you respect their preferences.

IF YOU'RE SUBMITTING POETRY, SHORT

STORIES, OR ARTICLES TO A MAGAZINE, MAKE SURE TO READ SAMPLE COPIES.

Many magazines have online editions now, so that's a good way to see the style of story they are looking for. Check your local library and discount bookstore for back copies of mainstream and literary magazines—it can save you time and money.

KEEP TRACK OF EVERYTHING YOU SEND OUT.

Make sure you have a written record of each piece and where you sent it. We are moms, after all. Time can get a little wibbly-wobbly.

EXPECT IT TO TAKE AWHILE.

Most publishing companies take 3-6 months to get back with an author, whether it be yay or nay. And we don't recommend emailing them every day to find out if they received it yet. Be patient and submit to dozens of different publishers to increase your chances.

MAKE SURE YOU INFORM EDITORS OF SIMULTANEOUS SUBMISSIONS.

And check with the company guidelines before sending them; some will not even consider them.

A SMACKEREL FOR INDIE WANNA-BES

Both Angela and Jamie are happy indies for now, so this is very near and dear to our hearts. So very dear that we have written a whole other book on it just for you, *The Busy Mom's Guide to Indie Publishing!* But for now, we'll touch on a few important subjects to get you started.

The first thing to do as an indie is to make a budget. Yep, it's time to sharpen your pencil and have that all-important discussion with your spouse. How much can you afford to put into this project? Cost is going to depend on how much of the cover design, formatting, editing, and marketing you want to do for yourself, as opposed to how much you can afford to pay other people.

Self-publishing a book can range from $0 to $5,000 (or more!), depending on where your priorities lie. Throwing money at a project doesn't always buy you sales. When you're putting together a book, money can flow faster than lemonade at a 4th of July picnic. So it's best to be aware of costs beforehand and decide how much you want to spend on what.

EDITING: $50-$3,000+

Editing costs will depend on how much your writing skills have been refined through critique groups and practice, the types of editors you choose, and how many different editors you hire. Editors' rates can vary wildly depending on their qualifications—a college student might ask for $50 for a proofreading, while a well-known editor might charge $500. Also, most editors charge by the word or page,so a 30,000 word novella will cost less than an 110,000 word epic fantasy.

Here are some estimated ranges for the different types of editing:

- Developmental/Substantive: $100-$4,000
- Copy/Line edits: $150-$2,000
- Proofing: $50-$500

If you're just getting started, remember that you might need multiple rounds of developmental edits to make a draft really shine. Please don't spend a fortune on an editor until your book has gone through developmental work, like beta readers and/or a critique group. You will almost certainly lose money and waste your time.

Now that Jamie did her time learning the craft (it took about five years), she's gathered awesome alpha and beta readers and found editors who enjoy working for her at a discount. Because of this, she doesn't spend more than $1,000 on edits for a first book in a new series, and only about $300-$500 for books 2, 3, and so on.

Angela goes a different route. She uses an extensive critique group called Scribophile for developmental edits, then sends her books to beta-readers, then finally turns her book over to copy-editors, which are generally much less expensive than substantive (or developmental) editors. So she spends less than $200 for editing, in every aspect. But keep in mind, Angela has spent 28 years studying the craft of writing, reading books, and listening seminars. We aren't saying 28 years of study is necessary for good writing, but classes and craft books do help the writing process a lot.

COVER DESIGN: $25-$2,000+

This should be your top priority if you plan on selling books. If you want to make sales, *people do judge books by their covers!* Especially now that competition is higher than ever.

FORMATTING: FREE-$500

If you're good with computers, you might be able to handle the formatting yourself. But we're not going to lie, it's an absolute pain in the neck to get started.

The Amazon KDP (Kindle) program has an automatic formatter that can turn your Microsoft Word document into a Kindle book for free. But it will probably look like the monster in your kid's closet chewed up your book and spat it out. And sometimes that can create errors that a professional would need to fix, anyway. Angela had a problem with that, and Amazon flagged her book page saying that people had reported formatting issues. Yikes! KDP does have an ebook preview tool, but

"I started writing short stories until one—for a decade—wouldn't let go of me. I kept returning to it before realizing it wasn't a short story; it was instead begging to be chapter one of a novel. So I wrote it into a novel.

And then I queried agents to see if anyone was interested in representing it. Sixty agents said, "No."

One said, "Yes!"

My writing had made someone else happy, and that made me happy.

Still, I had a lot to learn.

That novel wasn't right for the market at the time, so I learned to write beyond one project... Four manuscripts in, a traditional publisher finally found a match with one of my manuscripts, and I signed a traditional book contract."

Audrey Wick

Author of *Finding True North*

sometimes books will look different on different devices. So it's best to make sure you have it formatted right in the first place.

Other ebook platforms like Nook have their own free tools on their websites for you to use, but most of them are known for being painstaking and buggy.

Paperback formatting is also a challenge. Going through the approvals process with your printer (which will probably be CreateSpace if you're going indie) can last weeks and rack up costly proof orders if you're trying to work out all the bugs yourself.

We recommend trying one of the formatting packages at Book Baby. It costs around $350 for their ebook and paperback formatting without having them print a bunch of starter paperbacks for you. They have a nifty quote calculator on their website at www.bookbaby.com.

Several other services, including individual businesses, will format ebooks for a price. If you decide to go with one of these services we highly recommend you compare prices and check reviews before you hire them. If someone is offering to format your 500 page manuscript for ten bucks, yeah, you might ought to reconsider.

If you want to give it a go yourself, check out Createspace. They have a free paperback template you can download with page numbers, headers, title pages and everything else already installed. But these still take time to figure out, just be warned.

You can also find a publishing program to help you with your formatting needs. Vellum is one of these programs, though it only works with Mac computers. InDesign is also a program that can help the beginner with formatting.

Angela has a Windows PC, and she just uses plain ol' Microsoft Word with the provided Createspace program. Jamie uses HTML formatting.

ISBN: FREE-$125

Every print book (paperback, hardcover, etc.) requires an ISBN, which is related to the barcode on the back. It handles the book's information for bookstores and libraries, like its list price, dimensions, title and back cover copy, and more.

You can get an ISBN for free through CreateSpace, or if you want to keep all the rights, you can purchase an ISBN through Bowker at www. myidentifiers.com for $125. Or if you're planning on making a career out of indie publishing, you can buy 10 ISBNs in bulk for about $300. Keep in mind, you will need a different ISBN for paperback and hardcover editions of your book if you decide to have both available.

Why would you want to keep the rights? If you decide to later on publish with a different distributor besides CreateSpace, you will have to use a different ISBN.

Also, if you use a CreateSpace ISBN, CreateSpace will be listed as the publisher on your book listing under "Publisher." So if you decide to publish your books under your own press name, you won't be able to include that in your Amazon listing.

Side note: ebooks do not require ISBNs. If you publish through Amazon, they will create a special number for your Kindle ebook for free called an ASIN.

PROOF COPIES/COPIES TO SELL: $2-$20 PER BOOK

One of the fondest dreams of most authors is to hold their finished product in their hands. And thanks to several wonderful online companies called POD (Print On Demand) printers, you can order as many copies of your book as you would like and pay the same cost per book, no matter how many copies you order (in the olden days, you would have to order a large number of books at a time, which is why traditional publishers ruled with print runs).

There are several POD companies to choose from, such as CreateSpace, IngramSpark, Lulu, and Book Baby. In addition to binding services, these companies also offer other paid services such as editing, formatting and cover design.

QUESTIONS:

1. Is my book completely ready to share with the world, or could I use another round of critiques? Or have I been holding on to it for too long?
2. How much can I budget to save up the investment needed to create a professional book, whether traditional or indie, to give it the best chance of success?
3. Am I ready to treat my writing as a career? What can I do daily to move closer to achieving my 10-year goal?

Thank you!

So, was the information in this book helpful to you? Do you feel encouraged? More informed? Strengthened? We certainly hope so!

We'd love to hear your thoughts about this book in an honest Amazon.com review. And if you'd like more information on indie publishing or book marketing, grab the next books in the *Busy Mom's Guides* series! We've packed them full of everything we can think of to help make your dreams of becoming an author a reality—avoiding all the hard lessons we had to learn to get here.

Thank you for choosing to read our book out of the gazillions of craft books out there. We're honored, and we're here to continue putting out helpful info in this crazy, ever-changing market. You can follow our journey on Patreon, where we post exclusive updates for our patrons, or go to our website at www.busymombooks.com to sign up for our email newsletter for giveaways and goodies.

Sayonara!

Angela Castillo &
Jamie Foley

Sources

CHAPTER 1

*AMERICAN JOURNAL OF PUBLIC HEALTH ARTICLE REGARD-
ING CREATIVITY AND STRESS*
   https://www.ncbi.nlm.nih.gov/pmc/articles/PMC2804629

DOMINICAN UNIVERSITY STUDY ON GOALS
   https://sidsavara-sidsavaracom.netdna-ssl.com/wp-content/
uploads/2008/09/researchsummary2.pdf

CHAPTER 2

*WRITER'S DIGEST POST ON AVERAGE WORD COUNTS BY
GENRE*
   http://www.writersdigest.com/editor-blogs/guide-to-literary-agents/
word-count-for-novels-and-childrens-books-the-definitive-post

*NEBULA AWARDS® ON DIFFERENT CATEGORIZATIONS OF
BOOK LENGTH*
   http://nebulas.sfwa.org/about-the-nebulas/nebula-rules

CHAPTER 9

THE BALANCE POST ON ADVANCES AND ROYALTIES
   https://www.thebalance.com/book-advances-and-royalties-2799832

THE BUSY MOM'S GUIDE TO INDIE PUBLISHING

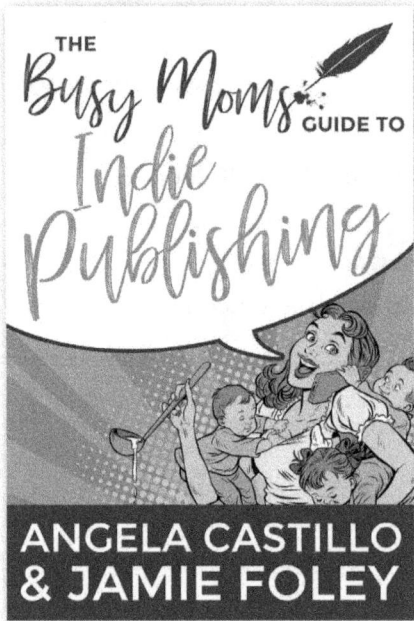

Self-publishing can be extremely rewarding, but it can also be confusing and frustrating. How does one produce a professional book that will sell for profit without breaking the bank?

This guide is packed full of advice from career indie authors Angela Castillo and Jamie Foley, including:

- Detailed instruction on formatting for paperback, Kindle, and audio
- How to make a terrible book cover, guaranteed (or not)
- Strategies for back cover copy, keywords, categories, and more
- Ideas for fundraising (other than bake sales)
- Marketing platforms that will form the foundation for your indie career

THE BUSY MOM'S GUIDE TO NOVEL MARKETING

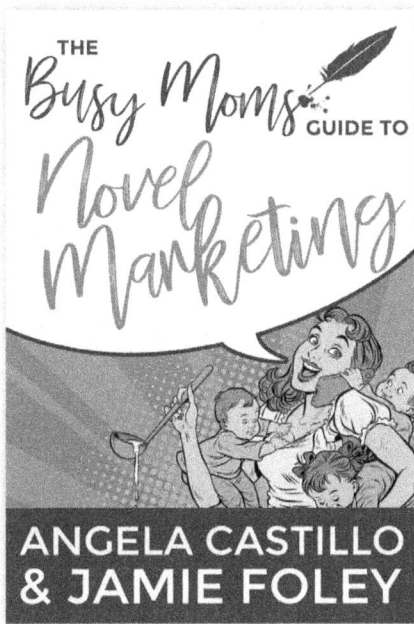

Marketing your fiction novels can make you feel like a small fish in an ocean. How can you get your book to stand out from the crowd—and actually make money?

This guide is packed full of advice from career novelists Angela Castillo and Jamie Foley, including:

- Which paid promotions and ads actually work (and how to do them)
- How to build your email newsletter list and social media platforms
- Tips for book signings, booths, and events (and digital events, too)
- How to get your novels into bookstores & libraries
- Giveaway strategies that will sell novels faster than granny's hotcakes

ASK THE BUSY MOMS

your questions

& CHECK OUT THE PODCAST ON

PATREON |

WWW.PATREON.COM/BUSYMOMBOOKS

Coming Soon!

SIGN UP FOR THE NEWSLETTER FOR THIS EXCLUSIVE .PDF

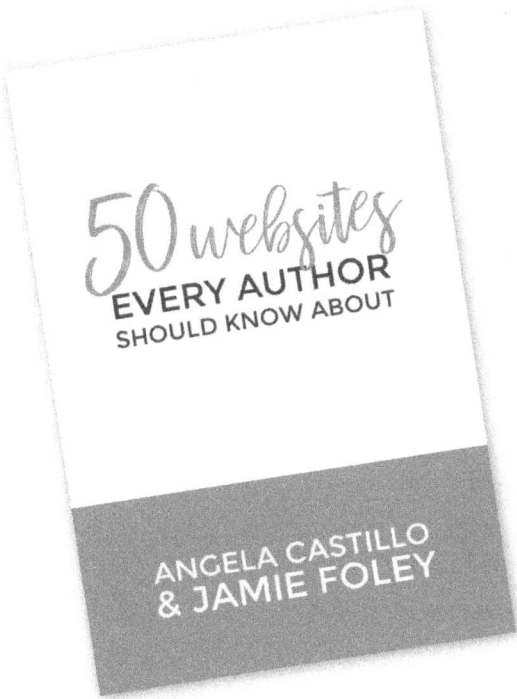

50 Websites Every Author Should Know About: Angela and Jamie's 50 favorite websites that have helped them the most in their writing careers.

free download!

WWW.BUSYMOMBOOKS.COM/NEWSLETTER

CONNECT WITH *Angela*

Angela Castillo has lived in Bastrop, Texas, home of the River Girl, almost her entire life. She studied Practical Theology at Christ for the Nations in Dallas. She lives in Bastrop with her husband and three children. Angela has written several short stories and books, including the Toby the Trilby series for kids.

WEBSITE

www.angelacastillowrites.weebly.com

FACEBOOK

www.facebook.com/adventurestobythetrilby

EMAIL NEWSLETTER

FREE BOOK WITH SIGN-UP!

http://eepurl.com/bLyYxb

AMAZON AUTHOR PAGE

www.amazon.com/Angela-Castillo/e/B00CJUELT0

CONNECT WITH *Jamie*

Jamie Foley loves strategy games, home-grown berries, and Texas winters. She's terrified of plot holes and red wasps.

Her husband is her manly cowboy astronaut muse. They live between Austin and the family cattle ranch, where their hyperactive spawnling and wolfpack can run free.

WEBSITE
www.jamiesfoley.com

FACEBOOK
www.facebook.com/jamiesfoley

EMAIL NEWSLETTER
FREE SHORT STORY FOR NEWSLETTER SUBSCRIBERS ONLY!
www.jamiesfoley.com/newsletter

AMAZON AUTHOR PAGE
www.amazon.com/Jamie-Foley/e/B00HJ8XIOQ

INSPIRING FICTION BY ANGELA CASTILLO

Texas Women of Spirit

Book 1: *The River Girl's Song*

Book 2: *The Comanche Girl's Prayer*

Book 3: *The Saloon Girl's Journey*

Bonus: *The River Girl's Christmas*

Toby the Trilby (children's series)

The Amazing Adventures of Toby the Trilby

The Further Adventures of Toby the Trilby

Toby the Trilby and the Forgotten City

Miss Main Street

Book 1: *Secondhand Secrets*

Book 2: *Blessed Arrangements*

Steampunk Fairy Tales
Multi-author short story collections

Volumes I, II, and III

Metal-Locks & Other Fairytales
A collection of eight short stories by Angela Castillo

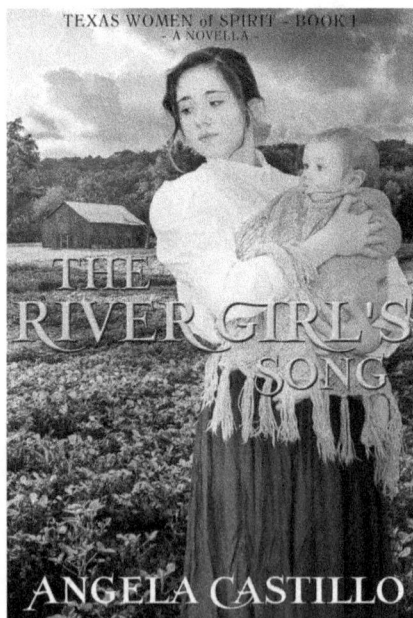

Zillia Bright never dreamed she'd be orphaned at sixteen and left to care for her baby brother and Papa's farm. With only a mule and a hundred-year-old shotgun, she must fight to protect what's hers.

Countless dangers lurk on the Bastrop Texas riverside. Zillia must rely on the help of her best friends, Soonie and Wylder, to hold her world together. With Zillia's struggles come unexpected miracles, and proof that God might just listen to the prayers of a river girl.

Clean, Christian fiction with a hint of romance.

THRILLING FICTION BY JAMIE FOLEY

The Sentinel Trilogy

Prequel novella: *Vanguard*

Book 1: *Sentinel*

Book 2: *Arbiter*

Book 3: *Sage*

Steampunk Fairy Tales
Multi-author short story collections

Volume III

*Coming soon: the **Emberhawk** series and the **Runes of Kona** series*

Blood-bonds with angels. Surreal mental abilities. Elemental gods.

The meteor storm wasn't such a big deal until a comet landed in the middle of the road. Now Darien's car is wrecked, his sister is bleeding out, and the only medical aid is at the reclusive Serran Academy.

Jet sees Darien for what he is: a lost teen who doesn't deserve to know about the aether gifts. And his sister's rare future-seeing ability is exactly what the enemy is after.

As fractured governments and shadow organizations vie for control of a dying world, the Serran Academy students—and their angelic secrets—are targeted for harvesting.

Clean young adult fantasy with fast-paced, epic adventure.

"Lots of action and suspense... brilliantly written."

— *Reader's Favorite*

www.ingramcontent.com/pod-product-compliance
Lightning Source LLC
Chambersburg PA
CBHW031627040426
42452CB00007B/709